ORIGINS OF ALCOHOLISM

STANFORD STUDIES
IN SOCIOLOGY, I
EDITORS

Sanford M. Dornbusch • Paul Wallin

Edmund H. Volkart • Joseph Berger

William M. McCord

ORIGINS

OF

ALCOHOLISM

by William McCord and Joan McCord

with Jon Gudeman

STANFORD UNIVERSITY PRESS

Stanford, California, 1960

OTHER BOOKS BY

WILLIAM McCORD and JOAN McCORD

1956 *Psychopathy and Delinquency*

1959 *Origins of Crime* (with Irving Zola)

STANFORD UNIVERSITY PRESS
STANFORD, CALIFORNIA
© 1960 BY THE BOARD OF TRUSTEES OF THE
LELAND STANFORD JUNIOR UNIVERSITY
LIBRARY OF CONGRESS CATALOG CARD NUMBER: 60-11629
PRINTED IN THE UNITED STATES OF AMERICA

TO GEOFFREY AND ROBERT

PREFACE

Men of every culture, in every historical period, have heeded Omar Khayyam's advice, "While you live, drink!—for, once dead, you never shall return." The physiological reasons are clear: Alcohol is a narcotic which can deaden pain, conquer anxiety, put the brain (and rationality) to sleep. The psychological reasons are, however, obscure: What kinds of suffering, experienced by what types of men, lead to dependence on alcohol? Why do some men resist the admittedly powerful lures of alcohol while other men succumb? How does it happen that several million men and women in modern America put alcohol above any of the other satisfactions of life? Various answers—social, philosophic, religious, medical, psychological, humorous—have been proposed. Yet these answers have been produced by studies of selected alcoholics, after their identification as alcoholics, whose backgrounds have then been reconstructed.

In this study, on the other hand, we begin with a group of boys and trace them to adulthood. Some of the boys grew up to be criminals, some alcoholics, and some never came into conflict with the mores of society. We compare the minority who became alcoholics with the majority who have not been defined by their community as "deviants."

In Chapter 1 we outline the approach of the study, and delimit the methods for categorizing the backgrounds of each child, for deciding the physiological, psychological, and social characteristics of the boys and their families; and define that slippery term "alcoholism." The problem of defining alcoholism is far from simple; Booth Tarkington once wrote: "There are two things that will be believed of any man whatsoever, and one of them is that he has taken to drink." We believe, however, that our definition of the disorder—which is closely linked to certain social variables—has the virtue of being open to scientific replication.

In Chapter 2 we examine some of the more prevalent theories concerning the nature of alcoholism. While these explanations run the gamut from endocrinological to cultural, they share a single disturbing characteristic: all of the research is based on an adult sample of alcoholics and, thus, is retrospective. Most of these theories fail to be confirmed by our data.

In the succeeding four chapters, we explore the early backgrounds of alcoholics. First, we separate some of the generally predisposing factors—parental conflict, neural disorder, certain types of social and religious roles—which, by heightening inner stress, pave the way for alcoholism. Second, we concentrate on dependency conflict, the battle within a person between his intensified need to be loved and his equally strong desire to repress this need. This particular conflict appears prominently in the character of the alcoholic. Third, we examine the specification of roles within the family; alcoholics, our analysis would indicate, are confused in their perception of role expectations. In Chapter 6 we dissect the interrelationship between certain of these diverse variables and alcoholism.

From this analysis, a consistent, statistically significant pattern emerges: the typical alcoholic, as a child, underwent a variety of experiences that heightened inner stress, intensified his desire for love, and produced a distorted self-image. We point out in Chapter 6 that highly accurate predictions of alcoholism could have been made simply on the basis of these patterns.

It is not sufficient, however, merely to differentiate the alcoholic from the nondeviant, for it might be argued that this same type of background leads to other forms of deviance. Consequently, in Chapter 7 we compare the genesis of alcoholism with the causes of nonalcoholic criminality. In a number of ways, the backgrounds of nonalcoholic criminals and of alcoholics prove to be similar. Yet, in other ways, the backgrounds of these two types of deviants are distinctive.

In Chapter 8 we examine the personality of alcoholics, both

in childhood and in adulthood. In childhood, the alcoholics appeared to be highly masculine, extroverted, aggressive, "lone-wolf-ish"—all manifestations, we believe, of their denial of the need to be loved. An analysis of the personality of adult alcoholics leads to the conclusion that the disorder itself produces some rather striking behavioral changes.

Finally, in the last section, we draw together the various strands of evidence in some tentative conclusions concerning the nature of alcoholism.

This book would not have appeared without financial and intellectual aid from a number of people and institutions. Financially, generous grants from the Ella Lyman Cabot Foundation and the Harvard Laboratory of Social Relations initiated the project; a significant allocation from the National Institute of Mental Health (Grant M2647) made possible its completion. We would like to express our deep gratitude to these agencies for taking a chance on the hopes of several young scholars.

Intellectually, we owe a debt to Professor Gordon Allport of Harvard and Mr. Edwin Powers, Deputy Commissioner of Corrections in Massachusetts and formerly director of the Cambridge-Somerville Youth Project. It was they who first suggested the study of crime (reported in *Origins of Crime*) and who offered important guidance and assistance in this subsequent analysis of alcoholism.

Ivan Vallier, Seymour Vestermark, Donald Tussel, and Jon Gudeman of Harvard participated in the laborious, sometimes harrowing job of collecting and analyzing data. Let us hope that this final result justifies the energy and resourcefulness which they devoted to the study. Jon Gudeman, now at the Harvard Medical School, played a particularly central part in the research. His intellectual originality led to the development of several hypotheses; his carefulness in analyzing the material served as a major contribution to this study. Those who read the brilliant Harvard honors thesis that emerged from Gudeman's work will easily recognize this book's debt to his thinking.

At Stanford, Allan Howard, David McCurdy, Emily Thurber, and Paul Verden, research assistants in sociology, took a hand in the final formation of the book. Barbara Little and Pauline Tooker, with their usual patience and good humor, unscrambled our writing and gave the manuscript its final preparation. Virginia Olesen, Judith Porta, Gordon Lewis, Carol Shumaker, Charles Oakes, John Rusch, and Stephen Anderson—all members of an informal seminar on personality theory at Stanford—contributed important insights to the research.

Information on the subjects' lives was gathered through the thoughtful cooperation of the Massachusetts Board of Probation, the Massachusetts Department of Mental Health, the Boston Committee on Alcoholism, and various Massachusetts chapters of Alcoholics Anonymous. We owe a major debt of thanks to the directors, staff, and members of these agencies.

Most importantly, perhaps, our gratitude goes to Dr. Richard Clarke Cabot and the staff of the Cambridge-Somerville project, who, twenty years ago, carefully gathered the original material which forms the basis of this research. Without Dr. Cabot's humanitarianism, foresight, and generosity, this study could not have been attempted.

This report represents another link in a series of longitudinal studies concerning the genesis of human behavior. We have tackled the problems of crime and of alcoholism in the Cambridge-Somerville sample. Currently, at Harvard, an analysis is being conducted of the origins of female delinquency in this group of families. At Stanford, research is proceeding on several varied topics, such as the familial basis of functional psychoses, the causes of high achievement motivation, and the sources of sexual deviance.

We are hopeful that these various studies will produce significant information about the development of human personality. Rarely in the history of social science do analysts directly observe a large number of people in their daily activities during childhood and over a period of years. Even more rarely can they trace the subjects to the beginning of their adult years. Terman's studies of gifted children and Gesell's examinations of childhood development are partial exceptions. The Cambridge-Somerville material represents another of these infrequent opportunities. Since this material is based on direct and extensive analyses of the early en-

vironments, since half of the sample were originally chosen for
their "normality" and half for their apparent "maladjustment," since
the data were gathered by a number of observers unaware of the
hypotheses to be tested—for these and other reasons the Cambridge-Somerville project should lead to greater understanding of
the role of childhood in the development of personality. Ulti-
mately, the aim of social science is the full understanding of the
person; we hope that these studies will be further steps in that
direction.

WILLIAM McCORD
JOAN McCORD

Stanford, California, 1960

CONTENTS

I

A STUDY OF ALCOHOLISM

Kenneth Gowan stumbled down the darkened street, clutch-ing a bottle of Burgundy. He stepped into a deserted alley and took a swig of wine. His stomach felt warm; a feeling of content-ment spread through him. He felt stronger now, better able to face the inevitable reproaches of his wife. He had lost his job today, which, he knew, would anger his wife. Overcoming his anxiety, he walked up the steps of his dirty, run-down apartment house. As he climbed the stairs he felt dizzy, but another long drink from the bottle steadied him. He straightened his tie, un-locked the door of his apartment, and yelled for his wife. The children were, as usual, out on the streets somewhere. And, as usual, Kenneth's wife exploded at the sight of his drunkenness. The fight that developed was merely a repetition of an old pat-tern. For Kenneth, however, there was always comfort at the bottom of the bottle.

Kenneth began drinking in 1948, when he was twenty-one. For many reasons, he had decided to leave his home in Cambridge, Massachusetts, to live with an aunt in Boston. His aunt and her husband were hard drinkers, particularly on their week-end binges. Kenneth soon found that he was expected to accompany them to saloons and to "hold his liquor." To pay for his "keep," he secured a job at the Boston shipyards. His native intelligence and a few months of training turned him into a skilled welder, charged with complicated marine jobs. On the job, too, drinking was common; Kenneth found that sips of whisky, at the end of a long afternoon in the yards, helped to overcome fatigue.

New Year's Eve, 1948, marked a crisis in Kenneth's life. Mixing gin, whisky, and rum at a raucous party gave Kenneth the biggest drunk (and the biggest hang-over) of his life. Later, he could remember little of what had happened that evening; he had "blacked-out." The next day, he confided to a friend that he was giving up alcohol; "I'm keeping away from that stuff," he had said, pointing to a bottle.

His resolution soon collapsed. In 1949, he joined the Navy and was stationed in Boston. He began to take secret drinks, "nips" from the bottles he hid around the barracks. One summer evening, he visited his aunt and her family. For many hours, they sat around drinking. An argument arose (Kenneth could not remember the cause) and ended in a fist fight, broken furniture, and a smashed door. Neighbors called the police who dragged a protesting Kenneth to the station. In police court the next day, he was put on probation with a warning to discontinue his drinking. During the hearing, his family protested that they were all good church-goers and that Kenneth should not be subjected to this disgrace.

In 1950, Kenneth's drinking drew official attention from the Navy. After repeated visits to the sick-bay (on diagnoses of "nervousness"), Kenneth found himself discharged from the service for "medical" reasons. After returning to civilian life, he shifted from factory to factory; first as a skilled laborer, finally as a menial day laborer. More arrests for drunkenness appeared on his record. Each bout with alcohol brought pangs of remorse; yet the guilt was not a sufficient block. By 1958, Kenneth's life had reached a low point; his job lost, his wife gone, his self-respect depleted, Kenneth took the final steps down the ladder of alcoholism. Now, each morning when he awakes, he reaches for a bottle; his drinking continues through the day. By evening, he is in a stupor; he has isolated himself from the community.

Why did Kenneth become alcoholic?

That is the subject of this book. Kenneth was one of 510 men of the Cambridge-Somerville Youth Study. First analyzed in the 1930's, Kenneth and the others have now been traced to adulthood in the late 1950's. We know, in rich detail, the early environment, the physiological constitution, the childhood personality, and the values of these men and their families; and we know, too, which of them have become alcoholic. Let us examine Kenneth Gowan's early background—as recorded in hundreds of visits and interviews over fifteen years—for the clues it may disclose concerning his alcoholism.

Kenneth was born on April 8, 1927, at the Boston City Hospital. His birth was normal; his infancy unexceptional. He was weaned at nine months and toilet-trained at two years. He entered school at six and achieved passing grades. His teachers described him as timid, easily hurt, "shrinking," greatly introverted. His hands were "clammy." He perspired generously when criticized by his early teachers and he often bit his nails when under stress. By 1938, however, his outward personality underwent a radical change. He became assertive, belligerent, and, according to one of his teachers, a typical roughneck.

This change may have been precipitated by his father's death in 1938. His father, a tough, red-faced, huge-bodied laborer, had sired eight children, five of whom died in infancy. He had spent much of his life in jail, charged with larceny, "breaking and entering," assault, and drunkenness. Completely addicted to alcohol, he frequently used his hip-flask. A history of epilepsy had been recorded on his side of the family, but he himself had never given direct evidence of the disease. With the coming of the depression, he could not find work and gladly gave up this responsibility, spending most of his time at home in bed with trash and bottles strewn around him. His death caused little sorrow in the neighborhood.

In January 1939, a social worker (part of the Cambridge-Somerville staff) unexpectedly visited Kenneth's home. His mother, distraught with the financial burdens caused by her husband's death, welcomed the social worker's offer of assistance. She showered the worker with complaints. She kept up a running battle with the landlady, who pestered her for rent. Her children had always been a burden; one surviving daughter had become a prostitute and the mother described the two remaining sons as "bastards." When Kenneth displeased her, she disciplined him with a broomstick. "I murder him," she said. "I get a stick and chase him. If he gives me lip, I bash his head in." In return, Kenneth despised his coarse, crude mother and opposed her with aggressive stubbornness.

In 1940, Kenneth's sister, the prostitute, had an illegitimate son. Much to Kenneth's anger, "Sonny" was deposited at his home. At home, Kenneth attacked the baby openly, but at school, his behavior changed back to the old mildness. He became courteous to the teacher, polite to his fellow students, and developed a strong interest in reading. His new teacher described him as very "good-natured," although she did note that he was somewhat "flighty." He dreamed constantly of being "superman."

By 1941, Kenneth began to show an interest in sex. His mother became actively disturbed, particularly when she discovered some nude pictures in his bureau. With girlish giggles she turned the photos over to the Cambridge-Somerville counselor and asked his assistance. Every week, one or more staff members visited the home. They seldom knew what to expect:

Item: In January 1949, the mother was drunk for three days. The children fed themselves and Kenneth picked up the weekly relief check.

Item: In February, the mother recovered her sprightliness. She smothered Kenneth with kisses and bragged about his continuing progress in school.

Item: In March, her antagonism to the boy returned. "He is a lazy slob," she snarled. "He's bound to get in trouble. He's a no-gooder, just like his father." As the mother made these comments, Kenneth (aged fourteen) sat in the corner, apathetically gazing out the window. "He's got no enthusiasm for nothing," the mother complained, "and those friends he runs around with are just a bunch of baloney artists." She whimpered, "he is so mean to me."

Item: In April, the mother saw the world through a rosy, alcoholic haze. Kenneth was back in her favor, but Sonny, the rejected infant, was getting the full force of her irritations. Neighbors having reported her neglect of Sonny, she was forced to appear in court to account for her behavior. A judge's warning accompanied her acquittal.

Subjected to his mother's irritable, changeable behavior, Kenneth avoided his home as much as possible. For a while, he frequented a nearby Catholic church and read widely in religious literature. His mother's disparagement of religion ("It just don't get you nowhere") eventually killed this interest. He sought street-corner friends and found an older boy, Frisbee, who became his mentor. Kenneth participated in various petty thefts with his friend until Frisbee was caught and sent to a reformatory.

Kenneth's older brother Al sometimes returned to visit his family. Kenneth was overjoyed with these brief experiences, but Al did not reciprocate. He disliked the boy and hated his mother (indeed, he was one of those who instigated the neglect charges against her).

In 1948, Kenneth left his home permanently. His contact with his mother was infrequent; he hoped to find new parents in his aunt and uncle. It was at this point that his addiction to alcohol began and it has continued until now, when Kenneth, aged 31, has become a confirmed drunkard.

From this brief history, social and physical scientists could draw a number of differing interpretations of Kenneth's alcoholism. Physiologists and chemists might point to several clues— Kenneth's alcoholic and criminal "heredity," the family history of epilepsy, the early signs of physical malfunctioning (e.g., excessive perspiration)—as indications of a general physical instability. By this approach, Kenneth's alcoholism would be interpreted as one symptom of an innate, physically based inability to function in normal society.

Psychoanalysts, on the other hand, might emphasize different features of Kenneth's life: the early signs of oral tendencies (such as nail-biting), his sense of inferiority, the early maternal frustration, the absence of his father—these, together with other aspects of his environment, would be regarded as most significant by the psychoanalysts. His alcoholism might be alternatively described as the result of an unresolved Oedipus complex, a drive toward self-destruction, a result of oral fixation, or, perhaps, a response to latent homosexuality.

Sociologists could well point to the values of Kenneth's Irish ethnic group, the role models offered by his alcoholic parents, the conflicting familial attitudes toward alcohol, the lack of social control of his drinking as the more important reasons for Kenneth's eventual addiction.

Psychologists might focus on the role of learning in Kenneth's life and depict his alcoholism as a natural response to his parents' patterns. Some might interpret the addiction as a way of compensating for the maternal love he had missed in childhood. Others would describe the addiction as a means for relieving aggression built up in the early environment.

Various interpretations of Kenneth's alcoholism can be found. Yet, one cannot be sure which explanation best fits the case. From one individual instance of alcoholism, it is impossible to know whether any particular explanation can be generalized to other cases. The major purpose of this book is to establish the basic regularities, the "laws" underlying alcoholism in modern America. By analyzing statistically the patterns found among the backgrounds of alcoholics, we hope to shed light on the problems confronted by a person like Kenneth Gowan.

HISTORY OF THE CAMBRIDGE-SOMERVILLE PROJECT

Richard Clarke Cabot, the founder of the project, a physician and social philosopher at Harvard University, conceived the Cambridge-Somerville Youth Study as a way of preventing delinquency and aiding "growth of character." Not content with the current practices of social welfare agencies, Dr. Cabot designed an ambitious experiment, from which three goals might be accomplished: (1) a relatively large number of boys would be given friendly and regular guidance by an adult counselor; (2) the effects of this guidance could be measured objectively by comparison with a control group of boys who would not receive such attention; and (3) information would be gathered about the relation between early environment and adult behavior.

In 1935, Dr. Cabot established a center for the project in Cambridge, Massachusetts. Hundreds of boys were referred by schools, welfare agencies, police, and churches in either Cambridge or nearby Somerville. To avoid stigmatizing the group, an equal number of "normal" and "pre-delinquent" boys were included. From a total of more than a thousand boys who lived in these densely populated, factory-dominated cities, 650 were selected for the project.

As a beginning, social workers interviewed the parents and teachers of each child. Each boy was given both a medical and a psychological examination. After a meticulous analysis, each boy was matched to another as closely similar in background and in personality as was possible. The pairs were equated in terms of physical health, intelligence, emotional adjustment (as judged by their teachers), home atmosphere (evaluated by a social worker), neighborhood, and "delinquency prognosis" (assigned on an eleven-point scale by a committee of judges who considered the boy's likelihood of becoming delinquent). One in each pair was selected, by the toss of a coin, to receive treatment.

Thus, 325 boys were to be given medical and educational assistance as well as friendly, regular attention from social workers. A matched set of 325 boys, a control group, were to be left to the usual services of the community.

A staff of well-trained counselors, drawn primarily from the profession of social work, were appointed to undertake the case load. In addition, psychologists, psychiatrists, and a vocational teacher were attached to the center, and other specialists gave their time when needed. Dr. Cabot had hoped that the program would continue through ten years of treatment; but by 1939, when the case assignments were completed, war was already imminent. Although counselors who joined the armed forces were replaced, the turnover remained considerable. Dr. Cabot himself died of a heart attack in 1939. Although deprived of his leadership, the Cambridge-Somerville project continued, first under the direction of Dr. P. Sidney de Q. Cabot, later under Mr. Edwin Powers.

Both because of the counselor shortage and because of the time-consuming nature of the written reports following each visit, sixty-five boys were dropped from treatment early in the program. For an average of five years, the remaining "treatment boys" were given assistance ranging from academic tutoring to psychological counseling. The intensity and caliber of treatment varied from counselor to counselor and from boy to boy. In some cases, as Dr. Cabot had hoped, treatment involved an intimate friendship between a boy and his counselor; in most cases, however, treatment consisted of talks between the family and the counselor, trips for the children, and medical aid whenever it was required. Many counselors, focusing on school problems, tutored their boys in reading and arithmetic; others acted primarily as coordinators for welfare and family agencies, the Y.M.C.A., and summer camps. Large numbers of boys were encouraged to participate in shop classes or informal games at the project's center. Religion formed an important part of the treatment: boys and their families were encouraged to attend church, and ministers and priests were alerted to the problems of these members of their congregations. Police departments, particularly the juvenile bureaus, kept in close touch with the project. All of the counselors made frequent visits to the boys' families to offer advice and general support.

Despite the concentrated efforts of social agencies and counselors, Edwin Powers and Helen Witmer found, in 1948, that the Cambridge-Somerville treatment had failed to prevent criminality.[1] In 1956, a second follow-up study traced the lives of these boys; again it was found that the program had failed to prevent crime. Approximately equal numbers of treated and of control boys were convicted for similar crimes.[2]

Yet, one of the most valuable legacies of the Cambridge-Somerville Youth Study remained: the comprehensive information gathered in a variety of situations, which detailed the everyday behavior of many hundreds of boys and their families.[3]

In 1957, we decided to use these records of "raw observations" for a longitudinal study of alcoholism. The Cambridge-Somerville material offered an opportunity, which has seldom been found in the history of social science and even more rarely in the study of alcoholism, to trace the development of hundreds of men from childhood to adulthood.

Of the 325 boys originally selected for treatment, the sixty-five who had been dropped from the program in 1941 as well as two boys who had died and three who were known to have moved away from Massachusetts were eliminated from further study. This left 255 boys from the original treatment group and their 255 matched mates in the control group.

DEFINITION OF ALCOHOLISM

One problem had to be dealt with early in the study: establishing a suitable operational definition of "alcoholism."

A primary distinction between the alcoholic and the heavy drinker must be made prior to any research into alcoholism. The simple consumption of alcohol clearly does not render a person an alcoholic. Yet, between the social drinker and the alcoholic lies a rather large group of "heavy" drinkers who could not be called alcoholic.

Some attempts have been made to distinguish the alcoholic from the heavy drinker in terms of dependence on alcohol. One difficulty with this approach, however, is that some people may depend upon alcohol—at least in specific circumstances—despite the fact that their heavy drinking may never become a problem either to themselves or to others. The second, more pragmatic, objection to this distinction is the extreme difficulty in determining who is and who is not dependent on alcohol.

Medical scientists are prone to distinguish the alcoholic from the heavy drinker by such physical or mental symptoms as cirrhosis of the liver or various psychotic manifestations. Yet few would claim that only those who exhibit these more obvious signs of alcoholism are alcoholic.

Social workers, in particular, have tended to emphasize behavioral symptoms, such as the inability to maintain employment or the disruption of family life because of drinking, as the distinguishing characteristics of alcoholics.

In 1951, the World Health Organization brought together these various standards of alcoholism to form a more comprehensive definition of the alcoholic: Alcoholics are those "whose dependence upon alcohol has attained such a degree that it shows a noticeable mental disturbance, or an interference with their bodily or mental health, their interpersonal relations and their smooth social and economic functioning; or who show . . . signs of such development."[4] Keller and Efron have proposed a similar definition:

Alcoholism is a chronic illness, psychic or somatic or psychosomatic, which manifests itself as a disorder of behavior. It is characterized by the repeated drinking of alcoholic beverages, to an extent that exceeds customary dietary use or compliance with the social customs of the community and that interferes with the drinker's health, or his social or economic functioning.[5]

Taking an abbreviated behavioral form of these two definitions, we considered an alcoholic as one whose repeated drinking of alcoholic beverages interfered with his interpersonal relations or his social or economic functioning.

Next, we were faced with the problem of establishing reasonable operational criteria for this behavior. Among some of the parents of our subjects we had evidence of alcoholism. Social workers who had visited the homes over a period of approximately five years had left comprehensive records of parents' behavior. On the basis of these records, parents were considered alcoholic if they had lost their jobs because of repeated drinking, if marital unhappiness was attributed primarily to excessive drinking, if welfare agencies had repeatedly pointed to drinking as the grounds for the family's problems, or if a parent had received treatment specifically for alcoholism. In addition to these more direct tests of alcoholism, we had obtained criminal records and social agency data on all the families of our subjects; some of the parents had been frequently arrested for drunkenness or had been treated by a community agency for alcoholism.

As a step toward settling upon the specific criteria for alcoholism among the subjects, we compared these two sources of data: the direct observations of familial alcoholism and the community records. We found that of the fifty fathers who had been convicted in court two or more times for drunkenness, only five had not been rated as alcoholic from evidence found in the case records. That is, 90 per cent of the fathers who had at least two court convictions for drunkenness had been classified as alcoholics from independent, directly observed evidence. Of the seventeen convicted once for drunkenness, the case histories of ten indicated alcoholism. Thus, only 59 per cent of this group showed independent evidence of alcoholism.

To ascertain alcoholism among our 510 subjects, we relied upon a "social" measure of alcoholism as defined by official community records. We gathered information on each of the boys who had passed through federal or state courts in Massachusetts or who were known to Alcoholics Anonymous, the Massachusetts Division of Mental Health, the Massachusetts Board of Probation, or the Boston Committee on Alcoholism.[6] From that information, we learned whether the subjects, as adults, had run afoul of the law, had been committed to a mental hospital, had contacted a mental health clinic, or had been in touch with a social agency concerned with alcoholism. Some subjects had, of course, been treated by social agencies many times (one man by age thirty had been arrested eight times for drunkenness). This information was kept separate from the data recorded during childhood; therefore, the staff working with the early records had no knowledge of the adult behavior of the subjects.

Equipped with this information, we established an operational criteria of alcoholism: Any subject who had been a member of Alcoholics Anonymous, who had been referred to a hospital in Massachusetts for alcoholism, who was known as an alcoholic by the Boston Committee on Alcoholism or other social agencies, or who had been convicted by the courts for public drunkenness at least twice was considered an alcoholic.*

Two criticisms of these criteria come to mind. First, by neglecting to include as alcoholics those arrested once for drunkenness and by utilizing only indirect community measures of alcoholic behavior among the subjects, we undoubtedly failed to tab as alcoholic many who should have been considered in this category. (By this rigorous standard, for example, only 60 per cent of the alcoholic fathers would have been included.) Second, because the subjects were in their early thirties, or before the average age of apparent alcoholism had been reached, we again undoubtedly "lost" some potential alcoholics. Yet, both of these criticisms point to the fact that those considered alcoholic in this study probably exhibited the most serious behavioral manifestations of alcoholism at a relatively early age. In effect, we had biased the study against ourselves, and could anticipate that significant relationships found among this group of alcoholics might well be typical of the extreme youthful alcoholics in American society. The major virtue of these criteria is that they avoid the ambiguity characteristic of other definitions and tend to exclude cases of a doubtful alcoholic nature.

By this standard, 10 per cent of the sample had become alco-

---

* In the sample of 510 boys, 46 showed no evidence of alcoholism other than the fact that they had been arrested once for drunkenness. The subjects were younger than their fathers had been when similar records were gathered for them and therefore, many might be convicted again for drunkenness; nevertheless we wanted to avoid—as much as possible—including any nonalcoholics within the alcoholic group. Thus, these 46 cases were excluded from the analysis of alcoholism.

holics in adulthood. Since half of the sample were originally selected because they showed early signs of maladjustment, this rate of alcoholism is much higher than would be found in a random, unselected population.

METHOD OF RECORDING INFORMATION ON THE EARLY
LIVES OF THE SUBJECTS

The records for the two groups, treatment and control, differed considerably. For the treatment boys, running reports had been kept from the first interview (between 1935 and 1939) to cessation of treatment (for the majority of boys, not until 1945). For the control boys, records had been kept of the original home visits and the physical and psychological examinations of the boys. In addition, records of at least three interviews and annual teachers' reports had been gathered on each of the boys in the control group.

Because of their greater validity, the treatment records form the primary source for this research.[7] These records give, in raw form, precise and detailed descriptions of behavior and verbatim reports of conversations. The families were visited usually weekly or bimonthly and visits continued for a median of five and three-quarter years. The counselor-observers, except for one who was a nurse, were trained social workers. They described in detail whatever activities they observed in the home, at school, during chance meetings on the streets, and in the Cambridge-Somerville Youth Study center. They reported conversations with parents, friends, neighbors, teachers, and, of course, the subjects themselves. Counselor turnover, considered a potential disadvantage for treatment, proved an advantage for research: the vast majority of subjects were observed by from two to four counselors. In addition, the records included information from all medical examinations, school data, records of psychiatric interviews, and reports from summer camps, Y.M.C.A. directors, police, and other agencies who had contact with the subjects.

The control records were used only to a limited extent. In some areas (e.g., birthplace and age of the parents), where the information between the treatment and the control records would be comparable, both groups were used. For most of the analyses, however, primary emphasis was placed upon the more detailed and undoubtedly more valid treatment records. In the Appendix, the data for the control group are briefly presented.

Before beginning the study of the 255 treated cases, we had to check whether the Cambridge-Somerville treatment had lowered the rate of alcoholism among the subjects. If the treatment had actually changed the rate of alcoholism, it might well have obscured causal relationships and it would have to be regarded as an important variable in itself. To check this possibility, we compared the alcoholism of the treatment and of the control groups.

A subject was considered an alcoholic according to the criteria set forth above. He was considered a "one-arrest drinker" if he had been arrested only once for drunkenness and gave no other indications of alcoholism. He was considered criminal if he had been convicted by the courts for assault, theft, or sexual offenses. The following tabulation presents the comparative rates of alcoholism and crime between the treatment and the control groups.

RATES OF ALCOHOLISM AND CRIME IN THE TREATMENT
AND CONTROL GROUPS
(*Number of boys*)

	Treatment Group	Control Group
Alcoholic, noncriminal	11	10
Alcoholic, criminal	18	12
One-arrest drinker, noncriminal	10	12
One-arrest drinker, criminal	14	10
Criminal, nonalcoholic	44	44
Neither criminal nor alcoholic	158	167

A total of 29 treatment boys and 22 control boys had become alcoholics; it is clear, therefore, that treatment did not deter alcoholism. After combing the extensive literature, we began compiling hypotheses concerning the genesis of the problem. By autumn of 1957, we had gathered theories that ranged from the purely sociological to the Freudian and the physiological. The second task was to make a realistic appraisal of the records.

Because the records had not been written to analyze the origins of alcoholism, we could not test some of the theories found in the literature. And because the records were not based on structured interviews, we had information about some boys but not about others. Yet, even these disadvantages had their advantageous side.

(1) The reports were written without theoretical orientation, i.e., without knowledge of the use to which they would be put, so no systematic biases contaminated the reports. (2) The information was gathered by direct observation and informal interaction over an extended period of time, thereby avoiding the inadequacies of self-report techniques and interviews.

Of course, the primary virtue of the Cambridge-Somerville records for a study of alcoholism rests upon the fact that the information reported had been gathered long before any evidence of alcoholism could have appeared. The boys had averaged nine years in age when the first observations were made; they had averaged eleven at the time when regular visits (treatment) began; and, on the average, they were in their middle teens when they were last seen.

Next, we worked out a comprehensive coding system which rated specific variables in several ways. This coding sheet consisted of about twice as many items as were finally used. At least two researchers read and rated 15 cases. Then every item was discussed. We discarded some, modified others, and clarified the remainder to reach high reliability in the final ratings. We attempted to use items that classified specific behavior or attitudes so that after we had analyzed the material we would be able to know what had been found. Thus, for instance, we omitted the heterogeneous classification of "maternal overprotection" in favor of separate ratings regarding the mother's affectional attitude toward her son and her restrictiveness of the child's activities. Also, whenever possible, categories were defined in terms of direct behavioral evidence. Thus, for example, the categorization of "marked femininity" depended upon evidence that the boy played with dolls as an adolescent, wore dresses, or frequently expressed a wish to be a girl. For these reasons, too, we used behavior as a test for oral tendencies (thumb-sucking, excessive smoking, playing with the mouth, and orgies of eating). We eliminated items for which no specific criteria seemed satisfactory, and we provided for the possibility of finding insufficient information in the records regarding any form of classification.

During the next weeks, a constant analysis, using the new code sheet, was made to insure that all workers had a similar understanding of the variables. The six trained readers were assigned specific cases from the files. Each case was, of course, read individually and recorded on a separate coding sheet. A random sample of thirty treatment cases and twenty-five control cases were selected for an inter-rater reliability check. For these cases, a second reader gave an independent rating on every item. Inter-rater reliability was high; specific figures for each category are reported in the Appendix.

The data recorded are composed of the following information from the case files:

1. Socio-economic and cultural factors:
   a) Racial background
   b) Religion of parents (affiliation and regularity of worship practices)
   c) Father's birthplace
   d) Presence or absence of ethnic maladjustment of immigrant parents
   e) Subgroup solidarity (with particular reference to minority groups)
   f) Father's occupation (position held and nature of the occupation with respect to the bureaucratic-entrepreneurial dichotomy)
   g) Regularity of father's employment
   h) Extent of the formal education of each parent
   i) Neighborhood of the home (residential or transitional)

2. Family structure:
   a) Parental unit (if severed, cause of parental absence and the boy's age at the time of the break)
   b) Number and sex of siblings
   c) Ordinal position of the boy
   d) Age difference between the boy and his siblings

3. Family interaction:
   a) Parental dominance (father, mother, or divided almost equally)
   b) Role of each parent in the family (as dictator, leader, "martyr," passive or inactive)
   c) Affection shown by the parents for each other
   d) Esteem of each parent for the other
   e) Satisfaction evidenced by each parent for the "role activities" of spouse
   f) Parental conflict (separately recorded for conflict about religion, money, general values, alcohol, and the child)

g) Affectional attitude of each parent toward the boy

h) Assigned role of the child within the family ("bright hope," "pet," "black sheep," etc.)

i) Frequency and nature of parental comparisons of the boy to other children

j) Whether or not an adult other than the parents strongly influenced the child's socialization (if so, whether this influence supported or contradicted the parental influence)

4. Parental attitudes and behavior:
    a) Social behavior of each parent (whether or not each was known to be alcoholic, criminal, or sexually unfaithful)
    b) Aggressiveness demonstrated by each parent
    c) Nature of social activities in which each parent participated
    d) Self-confidence shown by each parent
    e) Drinking habits of each parent
    f) Attitude toward drinking expressed by each parent
    g) Typical reaction to crises of each parent
    h) Value emphasis stressed by each parent (enjoyment, security, popularity, achievement, or status)
    i) Conscience orientation of each parent (other-directed, authoritarian, hedonistic, or integral)
    j) Feelings of grandiosity evidenced by each parent
    k) General body care of each parent
    l) Father's masculinity (in terms of interests)
    m) Degree of sex anxiety shown by the mother

5. Child-rearing practices:
    a) Mother's dependency encouragement
    b) Mother's independence encouragement
    c) Mother's encouragement of "masculine" activities
    d) Amount of supervision the boy had during childhood
    e) Mother's control of the boy during childhood
    f) Major disciplining agent of the boy during childhood
    g) Major emphasis of discipline
    h) Level of expectations or demands made upon the boy
    i) Consistency of discipline administered by each parent
    j) Disciplinary techniques used by each parent

6. Miscellaneous information:
    a) Presence or absence of sexual deviance (incest or illegitimacy) in the family
    b) Mother's occupation (if employed outside the home, regularity of such employment)
    c) Number of husbands the mother had
    d) Age of each parent when the boy was born
    e) Whether or not each parent had stomach trouble
    f) Whether or not each parent was psychotic or markedly neurotic

In addition to this background information, the following factors pertaining to the boy's health, attitudes, and behavior were recorded:

1. Health:
    a) Presence or absence of neural difficulties
    b) Presence or absence of glandular disorders
    c) Condition of tonsils
    d) Presence of stomach trouble or dietetic deficiencies
    e) Presence of severe acne
    f) Presence of body deformity
    g) Presence of obesity
    h) General body care

2. Attitudes and behavior:
    a) Ethnic allegiance (if the parents gave proof of ethnic maladjustment)
    b) Attitude toward each parent
    c) Relation of siblings during childhood and during adolescence
    d) Primary reference group
    e) Leadership among peers
    f) Relations with peers (aggressive, cooperative, or withdrawn)
    g) Degree of self-confidence
    h) Personality—in terms of extrovert-introvert dichotomy
    i) Typical reaction to problems
    j) Strength of desire for adult approval (other than that of the parents)
    k) Aggressiveness
    l) Destructive tendencies
    m) Suicidal tendencies
    n) Presence of abnormal fears
    o) Anxiety about sex
    p) Pattern of sexual experience (including premature heterosexual experience, "abnormal relations," and abnormal masturbation)
    q) Homosexual tendencies
    r) Feelings of grandiosity
    s) Nature of fantasies (dependency, aggression, popularity, success, or suicidal)
    t) Racial prejudice

3. Miscellaneous information:
    a) Nature of birth
    b) I.Q. score (Kuhlmann-Anderson Test)
    c) School retardation
    d) Occurrence of enuresis
    e) Occurrence of prolonged thumb sucking

f) Oral tendencies as exemplified by excessive smoking, playing
   with the mouth, or eating orgies
g) Energy level (hyperactive, normal, or passive)
h) Church attendance
i) Major problem in the home as perceived by the boy

Most of these items will be fully discussed and each will be
described in detail in the following pages. The complete coding
sheet is provided in the Appendix.

A methodological issue deserves to be considered at this point:
To what extent were the counselors' original observations valid?
Three pieces of evidence indicate that they were at least relatively
valid. (1) The face validity of the observation records is considerable. The families had been visited repeatedly by trained observers, the observations had been recorded almost immediately after
each visit, and the families did not know that records were being
kept. (As far as the parents were concerned, the Cambridge-
Somerville Youth Study was a "service" organization.) (2) We
found that certain of the more obvious biases did not contaminate
the data. One such bias is the possibility that middle-class "Yan-
kee" observers would tend to interpret behavior in terms of middle-
class standards. One might argue, for example, that a middle-class
person would, in watching lower-class behavior, "read in" aggressive intent where none was intended. Similarly, an observer raised
in an American milieu might tend to distort the significance of the
behavior of immigrant families. Yet we found no significant relationships between either social class or ethnic group and aggression. Nor were there significant relationships between high intelligence and "attractive" personality attributes. (3) Perhaps the
most important evidence for the validity of the observation records is the highly significant relationships they yield between
the categorized observations and the criminality of the boys as
adults. Thus, there is presumptive evidence that they have high
"predictive power."

*We would like to stress the fact that the original information
was recorded prior to the onset of alcoholism; that the observers,
though trained social workers, were not of a single theoretical
orientation; that the observer biases were partially canceled because so many reports were kept by such a wide variety of people;*

*that the observers had no knowledge of how their material would
be used in later years; and, finally, that the raters themselves were
unaware of the adult behavior of the subjects whom they rated.*

After coding the backgrounds of the 255 treatment and 255
control subjects, we recorded this information, together with a
coded report of adult behavior on I.B.M. cards. As a preliminary
to further analyses, we compared the six groups (ranging from
"alcoholic, noncriminal" through "none of these")[8] on a number
of background variables.

The backgrounds of alcoholic noncriminals and alcoholic criminals appeared to be closely similar; therefore, except in the chapter that deals specifically with the comparison of alcoholics and
criminals, we have considered alcoholism as the dominant trait
and grouped together all alcoholics. Because of the questionable
(alcoholic) status of those who had been arrested for drunkenness
only once, we omitted these 46 subjects (24 treatment and 22 control cases) from the investigation. As we had anticipated, the
nonalcoholic criminals resembled, in many respects, the alcoholics.
To distinguish the alcoholics from a nondeviant population, we
omitted the criminals from all analyses except those dealing particularly with differentiation among deviants (Chapter 7).

Thus, for the majority of comparisons, we considered the differential factors that distinguished the 29 alcoholic subjects from the
158 nondeviant (neither alcoholic nor criminal) subjects in the
treatment group. We used the Chi-square test, two-tailed, to ascertain the likelihood that differences were due to chance.[9] We
considered a relationship significant if there were less than five
chances out of one hundred of its occurring by chance.

SUMMARY OF METHODOLOGY

In 1958, after reviewing a variety of studies of alcoholism,
John D. Armstrong wrote:

The ideal experiment is yet to be designed and carried out, one which
will allow observation of an unsuspecting population, seemingly repre-
sentative of a larger society, over a time span sufficiently long to watch
the adolescent reach the age of social drinking which will eventually be
labeled alcoholic—all this to be accomplished without disturbing the
study sample by the process of observation.[10]

We hope that, at least to a large extent, this present study satisfies the criteria proposed by Dr. Armstrong for the "ideal experiment" in the study of alcoholism.

Between 1935 and 1945, 255 male subjects and their families were repeatedly observed by a variety of social workers, doctors, and psychiatrists during a long period of time (approximately five years) of their childhood. An additional 255 subjects were interviewed and observed less extensively. The subjects averaged nine years of age at the time when contact was first established. All of the subjects were cases in the Cambridge-Somerville project and had been selected for reasons other than potential alcoholism (half as potential delinquents and half for the "normality" of their behavior). Although the subjects differed from a random American sample (all came from urban areas, all were male, more of the subjects were social deviants, more came from the lower-class, more derived from immigrant ethnic groups, and more belonged to the Roman Catholic faith), their distinguishing characteristics have certain advantages for the study of alcoholism.

Ten per cent of the boys had, by their early thirties, become "alcoholic"; they had either been arrested two or more times for drunkenness, joined Alcoholics Anonymous, or had come into contact with a social agency or mental hospital charged with the treatment of alcoholism. Although this operational standard of alcoholism omits those who have not been defined by their community as alcoholic, it does encompass those whose excessive drinking has brought them into serious conflict with their society.

The social, familial, psychological, and physiological background of both the alcoholics and a "normal" group of subjects (neither alcoholic, nor criminal, nor arrested for drunkenness) was categorized. Information on the physical status and intelligence of the subjects came from a series of investigations made by physicians, psychologists, and psychiatrists. Information on the familial background, childhood personality, and social milieu of the subjects was derived from direct observations made by the staff of the Cambridge-Somerville project. These observations were detailed, extensive, and relatively free from preconceived biases, for the observations were recorded in "raw" form by a number of different observers stemming from a variety of theo-

retical traditions. Moreover, the observers had no knowledge of
the adult lives of the boys and no knowledge of the purpose to
which their observations would be put. The observers had an
opportunity to watch the subjects and their families over an average of more than five years.

These raw observations were then rated into discrete, largely
behaviorally defined categorizations. *The raters had no knowledge about which of their subjects were alcoholic and which were
nonalcoholic.* Rigid definitions of the categories and repeated
tests of inter-rater agreement resulted in a relatively high degree
of reliability and, presumably, the elimination of "the halo effect"
in rating.

Since it represents the first longitudinal study of the genesis of
alcoholism, this study has, we believe, particular relevance to the
evaluation of current theories.[11] In the next chapter, therefore,
we present an empirical evaluation of some of the current popular
explanations of alcoholism.

2

CURRENT THEORIES OF ALCOHOLISM

Over 4,000,000 Americans are alcoholics. Such a massive social problem has called forth many attempts to understand the phenomenon. Literally thousands of articles and books have been addressed to the origins of alcoholism. Physiologists and chemists have examined the physical condition of alcoholics, sociologists have unearthed the relation of alcoholism to a variety of social correlates, and psychoanalysts have been concerned with the dynamic, unconscious sources of the disorder. Most of this research has depended upon samples of alcoholics obtained after the disorder has taken control of their bodies and minds. In this chapter, we will review a few of the more common theories of alcoholism and subject them to an empirical evaluation.

PHYSIOLOGICAL THEORIES OF ALCOHOLISM

One of the more popular opinions about the causation of the disorder attributes alcoholism to a physically based craving for alcohol—a craving caused by nutritional deficiencies, glandular disorder, innate metabolic dysfunctions, or an unfortunate inheritance. Dr. Benjamin Rush, earliest American author of a scientific work on inebriety, first suggested a resemblance between alcoholism and either inherited or contagious physical diseases. In his "Inquiry Into the Effects of Ardent Spirits," Rush commented:

It is remarkable that drunkenness resembles hereditary, family, and contagious diseases. I have known it to descend from a father to four out of five of his children. I have seen three, and once four brothers who were of sober ancestors affected by it, and I have heard of its spreading through a whole family composed of members not originally related to each other.[1]

Today, theories emphasizing physical causation have become more sophisticated, more specific, and have some foundation in empirical research. One large "family" of theories concentrates on metabolic, nutritional deficiencies as the source of alcoholism. Roger J. Williams, former President of the American Chemical Society, is perhaps the most outspoken advocate of this position. Williams believes that a biochemical defect, a genetotrophic lack of nutritive elements, produces the disorder. In a recent article,[2] he reasons that certain genetic blocks lead to diminished production of specific enzymes, resulting in the person's inability to utilize some nutritive element. This defect creates a unique metabolic pattern whose balance can be maintained only by a steady intake of alcohol. Thus, according to this theory, stress in the internal or cellular environment, rather than the pressures of an external environment, causes alcoholism. Williams has offered a few studies of chronic alcoholics and experiments with rats as confirmation.[3]

Jorge Madrones, Natividad Segorua, and Arturo Hederra, all of Chile, experimentally bred a strain of rats that demonstrated a marked craving for alcohol.[4] These rats, inbred over seven generations, were fed a diet deficient in B vitamins. Their desire for alcohol increased. The experimenters observed the rats' voluntary intake of alcohol during this period. The experiment indicated a positive correlation of .41 between the alcohol intake of parents and their offspring.

Other investigators have followed a similar line of reasoning. William Sheldon, in his famous analyses of physical constitution, has found a positive relation between "mesomorphy" (a strong, muscular body type) and alcoholism.[5] Presumably, this can be traced to a genetic or metabolic difference between the mesomorphs and other body types.

M. Freile Fleetwood recently reported a series of experiments on chronic alcoholics, patients of a mental clinic.[6] He found a chemical difference between the alcoholics and a control group of nonalcoholics. The alcoholics had a greater amount of a chemical substance which accompanies feelings of resentment. The amount of this "resentment substance" was decreased by alcohol in alcoholic subjects more than in nonalcoholics. Fleetwood reported a similar finding for a cholinergic-like substance which accompanies tension.

Still other scientists have concentrated on endocrine malfunctioning as the basic source of the metabolic disorder presumed to underlie alcoholism. J. W. Tintera, H. W. Lovell, and James J. Smith, among others, have tried using hormonal therapy as a cure for the disorder. In spite of the fact that these experiments have not met with marked success, the investigators have argued that inadequate functioning of the endocrine glands produces the disorder.[7,8] Recently, Manfred Bleuler supported this opinion after studying alcoholic mental clinic patients, in whom he found the incidence of endocrine disorder to be higher than in the general population.[9]

This research has been widely criticized, the most prevalent attack centering on the possible confusion of effect with cause. Critics point out that alcoholism may well cause metabolic or glandular dysfunction, rather than result from these phenomena. The intake of alcoholic beverages each day, they point out, is bound to have a debilitating effect on the physical constitution. Studies conducted on animals have been criticized on two grounds: first, there is doubt whether animal consumption of alcohol can be equated to human behavior; second, there is the belief that few people (in America, at least) ever undergo the severe kind of nutritional "starvation" to which the animals have been subjected.

Our research offers an opportunity for partial clarification of the issue. In childhood, before alcoholism set in, all of the subjects in our sample underwent rigorous physical examinations administered by staff physicians. In half of the sample, the examinations were repeated approximately every six months over an average period of five years. From this material, independent ratings could be made of nutritional deficiencies, glandular dysfunction, and the general health of the subjects.

Let us attempt to phrase the physical theories of alcoholism in specific hypotheses and test their validity on the Cambridge-Somerville sample.

The contentions of Williams and his group might be summarized in the following hypothesis: A significantly greater proportion of people who, as children, exhibit signs of nutritional deficiency and metabolic dysfunction, will, as adults, become alcoholic. The following tabulation tests part of this hypothesis on the Cambridge-Somerville sample:

NUTRITIONAL DEFICIENCY AND ALCOHOLISM

	Per Cent Who Became Alcoholics
Nutritional deficiencies present (N: 28)	11
No nutritional deficiencies (N: 159)	16

Obviously, the boys suffering from nutritional deficiencies did not have a greater propensity to alcoholism. Thus, our evidence fails to confirm the nutritional theories of alcoholism.

It can be argued, of course, that the gross physical examinations to which the boys were submitted would not reveal the subtle nutritional differences the adherents of this position postulate. Yet one would expect that if the theory were correct, even crude tests which identified only subjects with gross nutritional deficiencies should show a positive relationship to alcoholism. Nevertheless, the available data do not lend confirmation to the theory.

Next, let us evaluate the more specific, but related, position that glandular abnormality produces alcoholism. While the boys in the study were not generally subjected to direct tests of glandular function, the physicians identified the ones who exhibited obvious signs of glandular disorder (hyperthyroidism, diabetes mellitus, etc.). Thus, many of the boys represented the extreme end of the metabolic spectrum. The beliefs of Tintera, Lovell, Smith, and Bleuler, advocates of a glandular interpretation, can be stated in this hypothesis: Children suffering from glandular disorder will, as adults, have a significantly greater tendency to become alcoholic. Our evidence is in direct contradiction:

GLANDULAR DISORDER AND ALCOHOLISM

	Per Cent Who Became Alcoholics
Glandular disorder present (N: 21)	0
No glandular disorder (N: 166)	17

Substantially fewer children who had glandular disorders became alcoholic in adulthood.[10] While we find it difficult to believe that glandular disorder actually deters alcoholism, the evidence certainly does not support the opposite proposition. For our sample, therefore, the metabolic theories of alcoholism fail to aid in understanding the genesis of the disorder. (It should be noted, in qualification, that certain theorists maintain that diabetes is actually negatively correlated with alcoholism and, thus, should not be included as a "glandular" disorder.)

A number of scientists have postulated a hereditary basis of alcoholism. As their prime source of evidence, they cite numerous studies indicating that alcoholics are very often raised by alcoholic parents. E. M. Jellinek has reviewed these varied studies. From a total sample of 4,372 chronic alcoholics, Jellinek noted that 52 per cent had been reared by one or more alcoholic parents. Jellinek also pointed out that fifteen studies of alcoholics indicated an average of 35 per cent had been submitted to a "hereditary liability"; exclusive of alcoholic parentage, 35 per cent of this sample had deviant (criminal, psychotic, and so on) parentage. Backed by this evidence, Jellinek concluded: "The only permissible conclusion is that not a disposition toward alcoholism is inherited but rather a constitution involving such instability as does not offer sufficient resistance to the social risks of inebriety."[11] While Jellinek stated that the "hereditary factor" does not become operative without other "social factors," he found evidence indicating a possible constitutional basis. More recently, Manfred Bleuler examined 50 upper-class alcoholic patients at the Payne-Whitney Clinic, and found that a high proportion had alcoholic relatives.[12]

Proponents of the hereditary position do not argue that alcohol damages the sperm or ovum cells; evidence from animal studies has failed to support such a theory. Rather they postulate an inherited nonspecific "instability," which under certain conditions will result in alcoholism.

Critics of this position argue that it is impossible, in these studies, to separate environmental from hereditary influences. It seems equally plausible to argue that children imitate, rather than inherit, their parents' alcoholism. Impressive support for the environmental theory comes from the research of Ann Roe. She selected 61 subjects who had been committed to foster homes by the New York State Charities Aid Association. Twenty-five of these white, non-Jewish subjects came from "normal" parentage. Thirty-six others had at least one alcoholic parent. All of the children had been placed in foster homes before the age of ten. Roe followed up the children between the ages of twenty-one and thirty. She carried out extensive interviews with the foster parents and many of the children themselves. If the hereditary proposition were valid, one would expect to find that a high proportion of the offspring of alcoholic parentage would have become alcoholics. If, on the other hand, environmental association with an alcoholic model were the precipitating factor, one would expect that the children of alcoholics—once removed from their original environment—would not have a significantly higher rate of the disorder. Roe's findings represent a serious criticism of the hereditary hypothesis:

The children of alcoholic parentage . . . cannot be said to have turned out as expected on the basis of any hypothesis of hereditary taint. Of these children, none is an alcoholic and only three use alcoholic beverages regularly. . . . We must conclude that the reported high incidence of alcoholism . . . in the offspring of alcoholics is not explicable on the basis of any hereditary factor . . .[13]

Thus, Roe's evidence strongly suggests that any correlation between a child's behavior and his parents' alcoholism must be explained in terms of imitation, "identification," or "role theory," rather than in terms of heredity.

In our sample, too, a nonsignificant trend linked a son's alcoholism with his father's. Fifty-one fathers in the research were themselves alcoholic; a higher proportion of their sons succumbed to the disorder:

FATHER'S ALCOHOLISM AND SON'S ALCOHOLISM

	Per Cent Who Became Alcoholics
Alcoholic father (N: 51)	22
Nonalcoholic father (N: 126)	12

The tendency for the son to follow his father's pattern is not statistically significant. Furthermore, we found that alcoholism was more strongly related to paternal criminality (31 per cent of the sons of criminals had become alcoholics), a fact that supports an environmental rather than a hereditary explanation.

In summary, our research suggests (1) that metabolic disturbances are not significantly related to alcoholism; (2) that glandular disorder does not lead to alcoholism; and (3) that evidence for a hereditary explanation of the disorder is lacking.

PSYCHOLOGICAL THEORIES OF ALCOHOLISM

Increasingly, science has abandoned physical explanations of alcoholism and has turned instead to the theories proposed by psychology, particularly by psychoanalysis. Like physical interpretations, psychological theories draw their evidence from the analysis of *post-hoc* samples—alcoholics who have already been committed to a mental hospital or who have already approached a clinic for psychotherapy. From the psychoanalytic couch have come three major theories of alcoholism. (1) The Freudians have attributed alcoholism to one of three unconscious tendencies (or to a combination of the three): self-destructive urges, oral fixation, and latent homosexuality. (2) The Adlerians have explained alcoholism as a striving for power, a reaction to a pervasive feeling of inferiority. (3) The interpersonal psychologists, like Robert White, believe that the disease may be a response to a number of different motives, but most commonly to a suppressed conflict between dependent drives and aggressive urges. We will examine each of these theories in order.

Karl Menninger is the most famous proponent of the position that alcoholism is a form of self-destruction. Several separate explanations of alcoholism are intertwined in his theory. At times, he places major emphasis upon oral frustration; at other times, upon latent homosexuality; and at still other times, upon self-destructive urges. For the sake of clarity, we will temporarily postpone specific examination of the first two hypotheses and concentrate instead on the third. Since Menninger places prime importance on self-destruction, this opinion deserves an independent evaluation. The alcoholic, in Menninger's experience, is characterized by a strong desire to destroy himself; alcohol addiction represents one expression of this urge. The suicidal intentions are unconscious and emerge from a feeling of being betrayed in childhood. The alcoholic as a child was led by his parents to expect more oral gratification than he received. When his oral desires were frustrated by severe weaning, the child was overcome with rage and a desire to attack the parents. "The alcoholic suffers at the same time," Menninger has observed, "from the wish to destroy his love-objects and the fear that he will lose them."[14] Since he dare not attack the real causes of his rage, he turns to drinking as a form of oral gratification and as a way of seeking symbolic revenge against his parents. Addiction, in Menninger's opinion, is a form of self-destruction used to avert an even greater self-destruction. Again, according to Menninger, the alcoholic pattern should be viewed as a progression: frustration in the oral stage leads to rage against the parents; this rage is suppressed because of guilt and is replaced with feelings of worthlessness and inferiority; these feelings lead, in turn, to addiction.

No one can take issue with Menninger that alcohol addiction is "objectively" self-destroying; alcoholics lose jobs, disrupt their families, and run afoul of the community. Whether self-destruction is a causative dynamic behind their behavior, however, is a separate issue. We believe that the surest way of evaluating Menninger's theory is to examine the person's behavior before the onset of his alcoholic symptoms.

The sample was categorized into two groups: the boys who exhibited definite self-destructive urges (as shown by actual attempts at suicide, by repeated fantasies about suicide, or by threats of suicide) and those who did not exhibit self-destructive tendencies. Only ten boys appeared to have suicidal inclinations, too few for definitive generalization. Although the trend was not statistically significant, the following chart hints that self-destructive tendencies may be related to alcoholism in adulthood:

SUICIDAL TENDENCIES AND ALCOHOLISM

Per Cent Who Became Alcoholics

Suicidal tendencies present (N: 10) 30
No evidence of suicidal tendencies (N: 139) 14

The evidence from our study is inconclusive: Self-destructiveness may tend to produce alcoholism; nevertheless, the majority of alcoholics in our sample (88 per cent) did not indicate self-destructive tendencies before the onset of alcoholism.

In Menninger's theory, secondary prominence is given to oral frustration as a basic source of alcoholism. Other theories regard oral fixation as the prime motive for alcoholism. Otto Fenichel, one of the most prominent defenders of this position, argues that passive, dependent, narcissistic urges—an attitude toward life characterized by a wish to use the mouth as a prime source of gratification—underlie alcoholism.[15] One variation of this interpretation has been clearly stated by Giorgio Lolli in a recent article: "The alcoholic experiences unconscious and to a certain degree conscious longings for physical warmth, pleasurable skin sensations, maternal coddling, liquid and warm feelings in his stomach, which are not differentiated from longings for security, reassurance, self-respect, independence, and, at times, omnipotence."[16] The generalizations of Fenichel and Lolli are drawn, presumably, from analysis of individual alcoholics undergoing psychoanalysis. Other investigators have attempted to substantiate the theory by examining larger samples. Alan Button, for example, recently published a series of articles detailing the results of his examination of alcoholics confined in a California mental hospital. Button subjected the patients to a battery of psychological tests. Although he noted a pattern of motives and traits which seemed to distinguish the alcoholics, he gave first importance (in his list of causes) to oral fixation. He found that the alcoholics were characterized by "a pregenital fixation, as a result of which oral objects (the breast and its equivalents) are cathected as the greatest source of primal satisfaction."[17]

If this theory is not merely circular (i.e., "the alcoholic uses his mouth for satisfaction, therefore oral pleasure is the cause of drinking"), it must be submitted to rigorous testing. In our opinion, the theory can be best established by proving that those people who have an "oral fixation"—a fixation that shows itself in other ways than addiction—have a significantly greater tendency to become alcoholic. We categorized our sample according to the presence or absence of "oral tendencies." We defined oral tendencies as thumb-sucking (after infancy), excessive smoking at an early age, eating orgies, and "playing" with the mouth. Fifty-nine boys in the study exhibited this behavior. If the oral fixation theory were valid, one would expect that a greater proportion of these boys would grow up to become alcoholic.

ORAL TENDENCIES AND ALCOHOLISM

	Per Cent Who Became Alcoholics
Oral tendencies present (N: 59)	12
No oral tendencies evident (N: 128)	18

Boys who had demonstrated oral tendencies did not become alcoholic more often than boys who lacked these tendencies. It would appear, then, that the oral tendencies sometimes observed in adult alcoholics are a by-product rather than a cause of their disorder.

Latent homosexuality (closely linked in Freudian theory to oral tendencies) has often been cited in the psychoanalytic literature as the unconscious force behind alcoholism. Sandor Ferenczi was the first analyst to propose this opinion.[18] Subsequent theorists, like Abraham, have elaborated the theory.[19] Abraham maintained that the alcoholic underwent severe frustration during the oral stage of development. In consequence, he turned against the frustrating mother to find solace with the father. This over-identification with the father results in latent or overt homosexual tendencies. As a substitute for overt homosexuality, alcoholics express their deviant urges through addiction. The male camaraderie of the saloon and the de-inhibiting effect of alcohol allow them to satisfy their inhibited homosexuality.

Other scientists have disputed these theories. J. V. Quaranta, for example, subjected a group of alcoholics to two objective personality tests. He found no correlation between homosexuality and alcoholism.[20] Similarly, Carney Landis studied 29 alcoholics, 25 former alcoholics, and 21 nonalcoholics and noted no relationship between "homoerotic" trends and alcoholism.[21]

The Cambridge-Somerville sample offered an opportunity for retesting this hypothesis. The boys fell into three relatively distinct groups: First, a small group actively participated in homosexual activities. (Naturally, many of the boys in the study had some homosexual experiences during their childhood and adolescence. One small group, however, demonstrated open, overtly homosexual attachments to the exclusion of heterosexuality.) Second, a larger number of boys could be described as having marked feminine tendencies; these children played with dolls, sometimes wore dresses, or frequently expressed wishes that they had been girls. We can reasonably assume latent homosexuality was prevalent in this set of boys (although we cannot, of course, assume that marked femininity always indicates a latent homosexual trend). Third, the remaining boys were normally masculine (as defined in the terms of their culture). An examination of the adult behavior of these children reveals the following pattern:

HOMOSEXUAL AND FEMININE TENDENCIES AND ALCOHOLISM

	Per Cent Who Became Alcoholics
Abnormal homosexual activity (N: 6)	33
Marked feminine tendencies (N: 24)	4
Normally masculine (N: 166)	16

These results do not readily jibe with Freudian theory. The boys who were overtly homosexual most frequently became alcoholics (with only six cases, however, one can put little faith in this finding). In any case, Freudian theory would predict that the latent, rather than the overt, homosexuals would have the greatest propensity to alcohol since overt homosexuals satisfy their desires directly and latent homosexuals express them indirectly through alcoholism. Our results, however, are in direct contradiction: boys who were markedly feminine had the least chance of becoming alcoholic. (When compared with the normally masculine boys, there was no statistically significant difference.) We are forced to conclude, therefore, that our research does not support the belief that alcoholics have latently homosexual personalities.

Adlerians differ from Freudians in their interpretation of alcoholism. The school of "individual psychology" maintains that alcoholism is an attempt to remove profound feelings of inferiority and to escape the requirements of "social interest." From his experience in analyzing alcoholics, Adler concluded that inferiority lies at the bottom of the disorder. Sometimes this feeling of inferiority is openly expressed; sometimes, it is hidden by a façade of superiority:

Very frequently the beginning of addiction shows an acute feeling of inferiority marked by shyness, a liking for isolation, oversensitivity, impatience, irritability and by neurotic symptoms like anxiety, depression, and sexual insufficiency. Or the craving may start with a superiority complex in the form of boastfulness, a malicious criminal tendency, a longing for power.[22]

This description of the alcoholic covers a wide range of traits; let us evaluate only the major premise involved in the Adlerian position: feelings of inferiority, open or masked, cause a person to use alcohol to overcome his anxiety.

The inferiority feelings of all the boys in the study were categorized. One set of boys exhibited open feelings of inferiority; they talked to the staff about their fears, their sense of worthlessness, their inability to face the problems of their life, their anxieties about the future. Another set of boys did not demonstrate these open, conscious feelings, although, at times, they may have indicated passing feelings of inferiority. A third group were highly self-confident. Given the major premise of the Adlerian approach, one would expect that either the boys plagued by a conscious inferiority complex or those who were apparently very self-confident would grow up more often to be alcoholics.

FEELINGS OF INFERIORITY AND ALCOHOLISM

	Per Cent Who Became Alcoholics
Very self-confident (N: 16)	19
Moderately self-confident (N: 119)	19
Strong inferiority feelings (N: 50)	6

Boys who had conscious, openly expressed feelings of inferiority became alcoholic significantly less often than those who lacked these feelings ($P < .05$).[23] Adlerians may legitimately respond that alcoholics, even as children, hid their feelings of inferiority, and that, therefore, our measure is not a fair test of this hypothesis. There may well be truth in this observation; as we will show in later chapters, alcoholics are characterized by hyperactivity and aggression—traits that can be regarded as a defense against inadmissible feelings of inferiority.

A second aspect to the Adlerian position is the belief that alcoholism (with its attendant feelings of inferiority) is the result of childhood "pampering." Adlerians reason that certain children are brought up in an atmosphere of coddling and indulgence; as they grow up, they are unable to face the demands of society; they therefore develop feelings of inferiority and turn to alcohol to resolve these feelings. As Adler observed: "Such persons have built up their original character in a situation of great pampering, in which they were dependent on others."[24]

Many psychologists, not just Adlerians, hold the belief that maternal pampering and overprotection is at the root of alcoholism. To test this proposition, we measured two aspects of the mother's behavior. First, we categorized the degree to which the children's mothers encouraged dependency in their sons, welcomed "babyish" behavior, and rewarded the boys for hanging on to the maternal petticoat. Boys subjected to maternal encouragement of dependency should be expected, given Adlerian premises, to have a high rate of alcoholism.

MATERNAL ENCOURAGEMENT OF DEPENDENCY AND ALCOHOLISM

Per Cent Who Became Alcoholics

Strong encouragement of dependency (N: 70) 13
Moderate or weak encouragement of dependency (N: 104) 19

Boys conditioned by strong encouragement of dependency did not become alcoholic more often than boys who were relatively independent of their mothers.

Second, we rated the degree to which a mother restricted her child's activity. Some mothers wished their children to be dependent on them, sheltered the boys from adversity, selected their friends and activities with meticulous care, and generally restricted their independence. These mothers, however, produced a lower proportion of alcoholic sons than did the less restrictive mothers.

MATERNAL CONTROL OF BOY AND ALCOHOLISM

Per Cent Who Became Alcoholics

Overly restrictive (N: 62) 10
Normally restrictive (N: 58) 14
Subnormally restrictive (N: 59) 24

Thus, neither of these findings lends support to the Adlerian interpretation.

Another psychological theory proposed by Robert White and

others requires special consideration. Although White argues that no one set of motives predisposes a person to alcoholism, he assigns particular importance to two personality traits: a desire for maternal love and an urge to be aggressive. In *The Abnormal Personality*, White describes the person who is most likely to become alcoholic:

There is a *repressed* but still active craving for loving maternal care. There is also a very strong aggressive need, *suppressed* by circumstances to the extent that it comes to expression only in verbal form. Alcohol does a lot for these two needs. It permits the young man to act as aggressively as he really feels, without forcing him to assume full responsibility for his actions. It permits him to gratify his dependent cravings without forcing his sober consciousness to become aware of them. Alcohol thus allows him to satisfy strong needs without disturbing the neurotic protective organization that ordinarily keeps them in check.[25]

As the reader will soon see, the research reported in the following chapters strongly supports White's observations regarding dependency desires. It should be pointed out that the alcoholics in our sample were characterized by treatment which would heighten desire for maternal care. The evidence for these statements will be presented later in detail.

In this brief evaluation of psychological theories, we have reached several negative conclusions: (1) boys who showed oral tendencies did not tend to become alcoholic; (2) boys who were markedly feminine (presumably with latent homosexual tendencies) did not have a greater tendency to alcoholism; and (3) boys whose mothers strongly encouraged dependency were not more likely to become alcoholic in adulthood. Two tentatively positive conclusions can also be drawn from the data: (1) boys with marked suicidal tendencies *may* have been more likely to become addicted, and (2) boys with strong, consciously expressed inferiority feelings were significantly *less* likely to turn to alcoholism for relief. With the exception of Robert White's theory, contemporary psychological explanations of the disorder do not, on the whole, fit the facts uncovered by this study.

SOCIOLOGICAL THEORIES OF ALCOHOLISM

Sociologists have produced impressive evidence demonstrating that rates of alcoholism are significantly related to the social structure. The value placed on alcohol, its uses in society, the manner

in which drinking is socially controlled, are all culturally determined patterns. Albert D. Ullman has expressed the opinion of
many sociologists concerning the nature of alcoholism: "[If] the
drinking customs, values, and sanctions—together with the attitudes of all segments of the group or society—are well established,
known to and agreed upon by all, and are consistent with the rest
of the culture, the rate of alcoholism will be low."[26] Research into
three aspects of society—ethnic groups, social class, and attitudes
about alcohol—has lent empirical support to sociological theory.

Perhaps the most sophisticated research into the relation between ethnic group values and alcoholism has been conducted by
Robert Freed Bales, who has suggested that socio-cultural conditions affect rates of alcoholism in three ways:

> First is the degree to which culture operates to bring about acute
> needs for adjustment, or inner tensions, in its members. [Second is]
> . . . the sort of attitudes toward drinking which the culture produces
> in its members. . . . The crucial factor seems to be whether a given
> attitude toward drinking positively suggests drinking to the individual
> as a means of relieving his inner tensions, or whether such a thought
> arouses strong counter-anxiety. [Third is] . . . the degree to which
> the culture provides suitable substitute means of satisfaction.[27]

To substantiate this motivational scheme, Bales examined the
differential rates of alcoholism among the Jews and the Irish. He
found very little alcoholism among first generation orthodox Jews
and very high rates among first and second generation Irish immigrants. The Jews, Bales reasoned, have a ritualistic attitude toward
alcohol. Their low rate stems from the symbolic associations that
surround the drinking act itself. Drinking is done at specific times,
in connection with specific ceremonies — circumcision, kiddush,
Passover, and Rosh Hashanah. "Wine is sacred . . . The attitudes
toward drinking are all bound up with attitudes toward the sacred,
in the mind and emotions of the individual . . . This is the central
reason why drunkenness is regarded as so indecent—so unthink-
able for a Jew."[28] Charles Snyder has confirmed these views by
direct studies of the drinking practices of Jewish adults and students.[29]

Recent empirical studies have shown that the Reform Jews
as well as the Orthodox have low rates of alcoholism. Conse-

quently, some scientists have argued that the pattern of Jewish attitudes—stressing mental facility, poise, hard work, and achievement—leads to an absence of drunkenness.[30]

The Irish, on the other hand, turn to alcoholism as a way of relieving a series of acute needs. In the homeland, drinking and aggressive horseplay are the major activities of boys when they are not working on their fathers' farms. A convivial, rather than a ritualistic, attitude toward drinking is common. In America, the Irish immigrant faces severe problems of adjustment. The father, who had previously commanded authority, is reduced to a role of insignificance and impotence in this country. The mother often becomes the dominant figure in the family. Because the culture puts few blocks in the way of drinking, alcohol becomes a common means to resolve tension.

Other studies have also demonstrated a relation between ethnic group values and alcoholism. Giorgio Lolli has analyzed alcoholism in Italians:

The use of wine seems to grow with the Italian child, from a few drops added to his glass of water early in childhood to undiluted beverages of adolescent years, the intake increases slowly and progressively until it is stabilized at adult level. Episodes of over-indulgence tend to occur as isolated experiences within the frame of a healthy family life. These rather rare excesses are accepted without fear and interpreted by parents and adult relatives as almost unavoidable in the maturation process. Drinking is done primarily at meals with solid food so that eating and drinking of wine become inextricably connected and related.[31]

Drunkenness is rare and rates strong disapproval. Among the Italians, the pattern of drinking is so enmeshed in family life and is so clearly defined that deviations are obvious. Phyllis Williams and Robert Strauss have independently confirmed the observation that Italians are not prone to alcoholism.[32]

Research by Milton Barnett in New York has shown that the Chinese, like the Jews and the Italians, do not succumb easily to alcoholism. Barnett found alcoholism was rare among the Chinese because family values and community disapproval discourage outward signs of drunkenness.[33]

Jerome Skolnick, in another piece of research, examined New Haven police records to determine ethnic group rates for drunkenness. A comparison of the rates to the relative distribution of ethnic groups in the area revealed that the Irish, Negro, Slavic, and "native American" groups produced the highest number of alcoholics, while Jews, Italians, Germans, and Scandinavians had relatively few.[34] And David Horton, in a cross-cultural study of primitive groups, found that alcoholism was most prevalent in societies where anxiety was high and few substitute outlets were allowed for either anxiety or aggression.[35]

Thus, past research has led sociologists to the view that alcoholism will be at its highest level in ethnic groups in which tension is high and drinking habits are not subjected to consistent social control.

To replicate these findings, we examined the relation between ethnic groups and alcoholism in our sample. The boys were rated according to the birthplace of their parents or grandparents. In most cases mother and father (and grandparents) came from the same country; when they were born in different countries, it was necessary to consider which cultural tradition was most important for the boy. We categorized the boy according to the tradition with which he identified himself. Unfortunately, there were too few Jews in the sample to test Bales' hypothesis specifically. In other respects, however, our research generally confirms past studies:

ETHNIC GROUPS AND ALCOHOLISM

	Per Cent Who Became Alcoholics
Italian (N: 86)	6
Other Latin[a] (N: 47)	6
British West Indies[a] (N: 17)	6
Eastern European (N: 14)	14
Western European[a] (N: 41)	17
Native American (N: 141)	19
Irish[a] (N: 13)	38

[a] "Other Latin" combined Portuguese, French Canadian, Spanish, and Greek groups; "British West Indies" was entirely Negro in composition; "Western European" included England, Germany, Scandinavia, the Lowlands, and British Canada. "Treatment" and "control" boys are combined in this chart. The Irish, because of their unusually high incidence of alcoholism, are not treated as "Western Europeans."

Native Americans, Western and Eastern Europeans, and Irish had a significantly higher rate of alcoholism than did Italians,

other Latin groups, or British West Indians (P < .01).[36] Further
analysis revealed that the ethnic groups that had a high rate of
alcoholism differed from the others in a variety of characteristics.
Most importantly, the "alcoholic" ethnic groups had a greater degree of parental conflict, twice the proportion of alcoholic fathers,
and a higher rate of other kinds of deviance.

Next to the Irish, native Americans produced the greatest proportion of alcoholics. Seldon Bacon, having previously noted this
trend, has pointed out that the drinking of white, Anglo-Saxon
Americans is fraught with ambivalent feelings. Sanctions against
drinking are erratically imposed, powerful emotions are infused
into drinking bouts, and guilt often accompanies imbibing.[37]
Bacon believes that community control over drinking in America
is relatively weak. Perhaps some additional confirmation of this
opinion comes from a comparison of alcoholic rates of immigrants
(regardless of their original culture) and native-born Americans:

FATHER'S BIRTHPLACE AND ALCOHOLISM[38]

	Per Cent Who Be- came Alcoholics
American-born father (N: 90)	21
Immigrant father (N: 94)	10

Sons of native-born American fathers had a significantly higher
rate of alcoholism than did sons of immigrant fathers (P < .05).[39]
Perhaps the complexities, contradictions, and lack of control in
American society produce a generalized proneness to alcoholism.

Another explanation is plausible: Immigrants in general can
be regarded as relatively "achievement-oriented" people, anxious
to turn their children into good Americans. As we will demonstrate
in a later chapter, those fathers who imposed high demands on
their sons produced few alcoholics. Thus, it may be that immigrants attempt to inject a more responsible attitude in their children than do native Americans. This training in responsibility
may lead to the relatively low rate of alcoholism among immigrant
sons.

Many sociologists have remarked that within American culture
the social class hierarchy tends to pattern drinking habits and,
thus, alcoholism. In a well-known article summarizing community studies, John Dollard has characterized American class differ-

ences in drinking mores.[40] Dollard argued that the upper-upper class holds a tolerant view of drinking, condones it, and anti-social behavior goes relatively unpunished. Drinking is not a moral issue. In the lower-upper class, a "cocktail-culture" exists; drinking is aggressive and a necessity in climbing the social ladder. The upper-middle class, Dollard believes, is neutral in its attitude, but the lower-middle class places a strong taboo on drinking. Because of its desire for respectability, the lower-middle group condemns alcoholic behavior. In the lower classes, drinking is rife and relatively uncontrolled; open aggression often occurs. Although Dollard does not make direct deductions concerning alcoholism in the various social classes, it would seem to follow from his observations that the upper and the lower-lower classes in America would most likely produce confirmed alcoholics. Social control of drinking is weak and therefore excessive drinking could be one major channel for the expression of anxiety and aggression.

To test the relation between social class and alcoholism, we categorized the sample according to occupation and education. There were no members of the upper class in the study. We defined the middle class as those families in which the father had achieved at least a high school education and held a professional, managerial, or white-collar position. The lower-middle class was composed of white-collar workers lacking a high school education and skilled workers who had attended high school. The upper-lower class was made up of skilled workers who had not attended high school and unskilled workers who had been to high school. The lower-lower class, the largest category, was a group of unskilled workers who had attended elementary school only. A distinct pattern of alcoholism emerged:

SOCIAL CLASS (OCCUPATION AND EDUCATION)
AND ALCOHOLISM[a]

	Per Cent Who Became Alcoholics
Middle class (N: 28)	21
Lower-middle class (N: 36)	22
Upper-lower class (N: 116)	17
Lower-lower class (N: 138)	10

[a] Both "treatment" and "control" boys are included. Cross-runs of social class and such other factors as parental attitudes toward the child, parental behavior, family conflict, and discipline indicated that social class is related

The middle class and the lower-middle class produced a significantly greater proportion of alcoholics than did the lower-lower class (P < .025).[41] These results run contrary to Dollard's expectations. Apparently social control over the use of alcohol is not as free in the lower classes as has been described; nor, on the other hand, is the lower-middle class as strict. These results suggest that alcoholism is not severely punished in the middle classes and that drinking represents one major outlet for middle-class anxiety. One might argue, conversely, that Dollard's description of various social classes is accurate, but that social control, as such, is not the deciding factor.

These results are more consistent with those produced by a survey study conducted by John W. Riley and Charles F. Marden,[42] who found more drinking in higher economic levels and among high-school graduates than among groups lower in socio-economic status.

Familial attitudes about drinking are, presumably, one of the major ways in which alcoholism is subjected to social control. Several sociologists have suggested that parental conflict over the uses of alcohol is a primary source of addiction. Joan K. Jackson and Ralph Conner, for example, reported in 1953 that adult alcoholics regarded their parents as having had inconsistent attitudes about drinking.[43] A comparison of adult alcoholics, moderate drinkers, and nondrinkers indicated great parental disagreement in the families of addicts. This disagreement, in the opinion of some scientists, gives alcohol a "magic," forbidden quality and prevents the establishment of consistent internal control over drinking. Albert D. Ullman, following a similar line of investigation, has compared the first experiences with alcohol of alcoholic jail inmates and nonaddicted college students. The alcoholics, he found, were more likely to remember their first drink, to have taken the drink outside their family circle, and to have become intoxicated. Thus, their drinking behavior was not under familial control and their first drink took on a "magic" aura.[44]

---

to alcoholism even when these other conditions are held constant. Thus, one is led to the conclusion that the general values held by the middle class are, in some fashion, related to alcoholism. We would propose that the greater middle-class emphasis on achievement and independence is responsible for this higher rate of alcoholism.

To estimate the influence of parental attitudes about drinking on later alcoholism, we categorized the values of the boys' parents. The fathers and mothers were rated as either "approving" of drinking, "disapproving" of it, or as being "neutral" on the subject. (Unfortunately, the attitudes of a large number of parents were not ascertained.) The two tables below show that this variable does not bear a significant relation to later alcoholism.

FATHER'S ATTITUDE TOWARD DRINKING AND ALCOHOLISM

	Per Cent Who Be- came Alcoholics
Father approves drinking (N: 53)	15
Father neutral or disapproves of drinking (N: 10)	10

MOTHER'S ATTITUDE TOWARD DRINKING AND ALCOHOLISM

	Per Cent Who Be- came Alcoholics
Mother approves drinking (N: 16)	13
Mother neutral or disapproves of drinking (N: 40)	15

Even though the parents' attitudes apparently did not affect their sons' alcoholism, we hypothesized that overt conflict between the parents about drinking might create uncertainty in the son and thereby increase addictive tendencies. Consequently, the amount of conflict between the parents about alcohol (quarreling, disapproval of one by the other) was categorized. Verbal, parental conflict concerning alcohol did not significantly increase the rate of alcoholism (although there was a trend in that direction).

PARENTAL CONFLICT ABOUT ALCOHOL AND ALCOHOLISM

	Per Cent Who Be- came Alcoholics
Basic conflict in home (N: 20)	25
Some conflict (N: 19)	21
Apparently none (N: 89)	12

Since we had information on the drinking habits of some parents, we also examined the relation between alcoholism and parental disagreement about the use of alcohol. Where there was direct evidence of drinking behavior, we categorized the parents as excessive drinkers, moderate drinkers, or abstainers. Though we found sufficient evidence for this categorization for only a small percentage of families, an interesting pattern emerged.

PARENTAL DRINKING AND ALCOHOLISM

	Per Cent Who Became Alcoholics
Agreement: both abstained (N: 5)	0
Agreement: both moderate (N: 13)	15
Agreement: both habitual (N: 5)	20
Disagreement (N: 21)	29

Again, we found a nonsignificant tendency for parental disagreement about alcohol to be related to alcoholism.

This brief review of a few sociological viewpoints about alcoholism tends, in general, to confirm prior research: (1) native Americans and North Europeans (especially the Irish) produced significantly higher numbers of alcoholics than did other ethnic groups; (2) native Americans had a significantly higher rate of addiction than did immigrants from other cultures; (3) middle-class Americans are significantly more prone to alcoholism than members of the lower-lower class; and (4) parental conflict concerning alcoholism may produce more addiction. These findings tend to support the argument that consistent attitudes, consistently enforced, will prevent alcoholism.

SUMMARY: AN EVALUATION OF SOME CURRENT THEORIES

In this chapter, we have sketchily reviewed some of the more common opinions concerning the genesis of alcoholism. Some theories of the disorder have been necessarily omitted; research on the subject has grown to the point where no single chapter can encompass the great number of current approaches. Nevertheless, the reader who is new to the subject can get some indication of the scope and variety of contemporary research.

We have attempted, in addition, to submit these theories to an empirical test. Because relevant information was gathered before the onset of alcoholism, certain retrospective biases were automatically eliminated from this study. The results suggest several general (and, of course, tentative) conclusions:

Before the onset of the disorder, the alcoholics did not differ from a "normal" population either in nutritional or in glandular functioning.

As a group, alcoholics were, in childhood, *not* plagued by inferiority feelings, oral tendencies, or homosexual leanings more than "normal" men.

Certain ethnic groups, the American middle class, and perhaps American society itself, produced a tendency to greater alcoholism.

3

SOME PREDISPOSING FACTORS

AN INTRODUCTORY NOTE

In some important respects, the evidence presented in the last chapter conflicts with the current theories based on retrospective studies; many of the causative hypotheses advanced by the analysts described in the preceding chapter are not supported by the longitudinal data. In the following pages, therefore, we intend to report a number of statistical associations between alcoholism and various social and psychological factors. This material is outlined in a series of four chapters:

1. In Chapter 3 we report the variables that are related to alcoholism but also are related to other forms of social deviance. We treat these factors as "predisposing" influences that lead to deviance, but not solely to alcoholism.

2. In Chapter 4 we discuss several associations between alcoholism and the character of the prealcoholics' parents, particularly their mothers. We argue (although, of course, this cannot be proven within the confines of our data) that these experiences exert a general influence on the character of the prealcoholics. Specifically, we defend the position that these experiences heighten the prealcoholic's dependent desires (his wishes for unquestioning maternal care and comfort) and, simultaneously, lead him to suppress these urges.

3. In Chapter 5 we outline the prealcoholics' relationships with

their fathers. We believe that the most reasonable way to view the evidence is to interpret the prealcoholic's environment as producing "role confusion"—that is, the child's relation with his parents fails to offer him a definite, specified image of his future role in life.

4. In Chapter 6 we discuss the interrelationship between the three sets of factors—the predisposing variables, the influences productive of dependency conflict, and the experiences that promote role confusion—and attempt to delineate their cumulative influence.

Before launching into a detailed examination of these findings, we must mention several general issues concerning our theoretical approach:

In attempting to interpret the results, we often go beyond the information the data provided. We were furnished with three pieces of information: measures of the early environment, measures of the subjects' observable behavior in childhood, and measures of adult alcoholism. We lacked information in such areas as the children's unconscious needs, their adult personality traits, or the specific adult experiences that may have played a part in precipitating their alcoholism. In interpreting the results, therefore, we are forced to fill in these areas of inadequate information by making reasonable guesses about the processes at work. Admittedly, we go beyond the limits of strict empiricism, but in a subject as obscure as alcoholism, we believe that this excursion is justified. It may be worth emphasizing that this theory emerged from the data; it does not represent the assumptions with which we originally began the research.

In presenting the theory, we make certain assumptions which, in terms of the information available, are unverifiable. We assume, for example, the existence of a dependency "need" in the subjects and that this need continues to exert an influence on the prealcoholics, even though their actual behavior seems to be in direct contradiction to the expression of dependent urges.

Throughout the book, we make causal generalizations from statistical material—an approach that is obviously based on a series of philosophical assumptions. Moreover, these generalizations are based on a small sample, only a minor, and perhaps a biased, slice of the total population of alcoholics. We defend our approach in the concluding chapter.

Let us turn now to the specific findings.

Three variables in the person's background—the degree of parental conflict within the home, the presence or absence of neurological disorder, the presence or absence of sexual deviance within the home—were related to adult alcoholism. We consider these factors as "predisposing" influences—that is, as factors that are generally associated both with alcoholism and with other forms of deviance. The boys who were subjected to intense parental conflict, to neurological disorder, and to sexual deviance within their families stood a good chance of becoming alcoholics, but they also stood a good chance of becoming criminals (see Chapter 7). These influences are not regarded as directly productive of alcoholism, although they are highly correlated with other familial conditions which are directly related to alcoholism (see Chapter 6).

The strength of the mother's religion appears to have influenced the son's alcoholism. Nevertheless, religion — like social class — would seem to be causative only as it incorporates other conditions that are more directly related to alcoholism. Thus, family conflict, neural disorder, sexual deviance, and absence of strong religious orientations form a general pattern that, when found in combination with certain other factors, may have predisposed the person to alcoholism. Let us briefly examine the effects of each of these variables, reserving until later an analysis of their interaction with other influences.

PARENTAL CONFLICT

Social scientists agree that conflict within the family creates an anxious, erratic environment for the child. It seems reasonable to assume, therefore, that families disrupted by conflict would produce persons characterized by a high degree of inner tension. Such people would be likely to seek one of alcohol's most potent qualities, its ability to reduce anxiety.

Most of the families in the project had been sufficiently well observed so that ratings could be made of familial conflict.* Since

* Broken homes have been omitted. They did not produce a significantly greater number of alcoholics than did united families.

the social workers and other observers visited the homes at various times during the day and night, the usual façades hiding the tensions of family life were soon stripped away. We categorized the Cambridge-Somerville homes into three major groupings:

1. Families characterized by "little conflict" were generally peaceful and cohesive. The parents mutually respected the rights and feelings of each other. When arguments did occur, they seldom entered the realm of outright recriminations nor did they usually touch on basic areas of disagreement.

2. Families characterized by "some conflict" usually had a harmonious aura. At times, however, this atmosphere would be rent by serious conflict. Such conflict was sporadic, frequently occurring over some specific incidents (e.g., drinking, treatment of the child, a job crisis). These conflicts soon dissipated their energy and the homes would return to their apparent peacefulness.

3. Families characterized by "intense conflict" were blatantly and regularly hostile. Arguments broke out on a variety of topics, often ending in physical attacks, threats, and even temporary separation. Members of such families openly gave vent to their contempt for each other. The boys raised by the intensely conflicting parents lived in an environment where stress and turmoil were the rule, rather than the exception. One result of this anxiety-producing background was that boys from conflictful homes had a significantly higher rate of adult alcoholism than did children from the other two environments ($P < .02$).[1]

PARENTAL CONFLICT AND ALCOHOLISM

	Per Cent Who Became Alcoholics
Little conflict (N: 53)	11
Some conflict (N: 56)	9
Intense conflict (N: 48)	25

We know that parental conflict produces a number of different disorders, not just alcoholism. Disruptive conflict within the home may serve as a predisposing factor in alcoholism by depriving the child of a basic sense of security and by leading him, early in his existence, to view life as an experience filled with anxiety.

NEUROLOGICAL DISORDER

All of the boys underwent physical examinations. Usually physicians reviewed the child's medical history and subjected him to relatively cursory tests. At times, the examinations revealed serious conditions which required more profound analysis. Fifty-one boys, for example, gave some indication of neural disorder. Repeated examinations (and, in many cases, EEG analyses) showed that 15 boys were definitely handicapped by neural disorder; the remaining 36 showed some signs (either on the EEG or in the form of convulsions, tics, or tremors) of neural disorder. Since the period when the examinations were conducted, medical methods of diagnosis and the science of neurology have vastly progressed. Many boys who apparently showed no neural disorder would today be diagnosed differently. Nevertheless, the 15 children who were definitely tabbed as being disordered represented the extreme end of the continuum—today, presumably, they would also be regarded as neurally disordered. Since only a sparse number of boys definitely suffered from neurological handicaps, it is impossible to make a firm statistical conclusion. Nevertheless, a trend is clear. A greater proportion of those boys who suffered from neural disorder became alcoholic.[2]

NEUROLOGICAL DISORDER AND ALCOHOLISM

	Per Cent Who Became Alcoholics
No indication of neural disorder (N: 136)	13
Some indications of neural disorder (N: 36)	17
Definite indications of neural disorder (N: 15)	33

A number of differing explanations could be proposed for this apparent relationship between neural disorder and later alcoholism. Perhaps neurally disordered children are inhibitively weakened and therefore more open to the varied temptations of alcohol; perhaps the presence of neural disorder operates only indirectly by altering the child's relationship to his parents and to other aspects of the environment; perhaps neural disorder is only a reflection of psychological turmoil. It should be noted that neural disorder remains consistently associated with alcoholism, even when other pertinent factors are controlled. It seems reasonable to suppose that neurally disordered persons are under greater stress—both physiologically and environmentally—and are therefore more likely to use alcohol to reduce the stress.

Both parental conflict and neural disorder create greater stress within the person (a stress that is expressed not only in alcoholism), thus acting as predisposing influences in the genesis of the disorder. An examination of the combined influence of neural disorder and familial conflict reveals an expected pattern:

NEUROLOGICAL DISORDER, PARENTAL CONFLICT,
AND ALCOHOLISM
(*Per Cent Who Became Alcoholics*)

	Parental Conflict			
Neural Disorder	Some or Little		Intense	
Possible or absent	(N: 102)	10	(N: 37)	22
Present	(N: 7)	14	(N: 6)	67

The number of cases is too small to attempt a test of statistical significance. Nevertheless, the trends should be noted: The few children who suffered from both family conflict and neural disorder were most prone to adult alcoholism; children who had undergone neither influence were least prone to the disorder. It is clear, too, that both neural disorder and familial conflict independently tended to increase the rate of alcoholism.

FAMILIAL SEXUAL DEVIANCE

Two forms of sexual deviance, incest and illegitimacy, occurred in the Cambridge-Somerville families. Eighteen families in the study contained illegitimate children (in most cases, the mother's children). In seven other families, incestual relations (usually between father and daughter) had taken place. In the remaining families, there was no direct evidence of either incest or illegitimacy. Boys raised in families disturbed by these two forms of sexual deviance had three times the chance of becoming alcoholic as boys raised in more "normal" environments.

SEXUAL DEVIANCE WITHIN THE FAMILY
AND ALCOHOLISM

Per Cent Who Became Alcoholics

Illegitimacy or incest present (N: 25) 36
No illegitimacy or incest (N: 162) 12

Families characterized by illegitimacy or incest produced a significantly higher proportion of alcoholic sons (P < .005).[3]

Clearly, this type of disturbed sexual pattern either creates or indicates disruptive familial relationships; presumably, the child exposed to such an environment suffers from a loss of a sense of security and an inability to participate in normal affectional relationships. As later chapters indicate, familial deviance of this type is not only consistently productive of alcoholism, but is also correlated with other forms of adult deviance.

RELIGION

Strong religious training has long been touted as a preventive for alcoholism (as well as other social problems) and adherence to religion has often been proposed as a therapy for the disorder. Many studies of adult alcoholics have shown them to be relatively unreligious people (at least in terms of formal practice). Indeed, Alcoholics Anonymous—perhaps the most effective curative agency in the field—has a pervasive religious emphasis. Because of the popularity of these arguments, we thought it worthwhile to test the efficacy of religion as a barrier to alcoholism.

The vast majority of parents in the study were, nominally, either Protestants or Catholics. Of the handful of Jews, agnostics, and atheists, none created an alcoholic son. The specific religious sect to which the families belonged had no effect on their sons' later alcoholism: approximately equal proportions of the sons of Catholic and Protestant fathers became alcoholics (14 per cent and 16 per cent, respectively) and approximately equal proportions of the sons of Catholic and Protestant mothers became alcoholic (14 per cent and 18 per cent).

The religious people differed, of course, in the strength of adherence to their faiths. The profundity of a person's religious belief is a highly subjective matter, which is nearly impossible to evaluate behaviorally. We did, however, divide the religious groups into those who, if Protestants, attended church at least once a week, or, if Catholics, attended Mass once a week. Among Protestants, the "strength" of the mother's religion was not significantly related to later alcoholism. Among Catholic mothers a significant difference emerged:

STRENGTH OF MATERNAL RELIGION AND ALCOHOLISM
(*Per Cent Who Became Alcoholics*)

	Catholic		Protestant	
Strong	(N: 46)	4	(N: 17)	12
Weak	(N: 67)	21	(N: 52)	12

Catholic mothers who adhered to their church strongly had significantly fewer alcoholic sons than Catholic mothers who were only weakly religious (P < .02).[4]

Although the strength of the mother's religion was significantly related to alcoholism, we found that the strength of the father's religion was not relevant. The table includes only the families in which both parents were Catholic or both were Protestant:[*]

PARENTAL RELIGION AND ALCOHOLISM
(*Per Cent Who Became Alcoholics*)

Father	Mother			
	Strong		Weak	
Strong	(N: 37)	5	(N: 5)	20
Weak	(N: 21)	5	(N: 87)	18

The predisposing factors were found less frequently in families in which the mother was (strongly) Catholic (P < .01).[5] Nevertheless, alcoholism rates were lower for sons of Catholic women when the predisposing factors were held constant:

MOTHER'S RELIGION, PREDISPOSING FACTORS, AND ALCOHOLISM
(*Per Cent Who Became Alcoholics*)

Predisposing factors:	Catholic[a]		Non-Catholic	
None	(N: 36)	3	(N: 80)	15
One	(N: 10)	10	(N: 49)	16
Two	————		(N: 9)	44
Three	————		(N: 3)	100

[a] Only strongly religious mothers were considered Catholic.

Among the non-Catholic families, alcoholism rates rose sharply when more than one predisposing factor—parental conflict, neural disorder, sexual deviance—was present (P < .005).[6]

[*] Thirty per cent of the 23 boys whose parents adhered to different faiths became alcoholics.

In general, one would expect that sons of strongly Catholic mothers would also accept church ritual and be subject to its training. This training possibly accounts for the low alcoholism rates found among these boys. In Chapter 5, we present evidence indicating that role confusion is one fundamental cause of alcoholism. The Catholic religion, with its clearly specified demands, may tend to substitute for parental failure to delineate role requirements (see Chapter 5).

SUMMARY

Certain "predisposing" factors in the background of a person were related to the onset of alcoholism. By creating anxiety or by offering outlets for anxiety, these influences tended to promote alcoholism or retard it. Specifically, it has been shown that:

1. Intense parental conflict was positively related to alcoholism ($P < .02$).

2. Neural disorder, especially in combination with intense family conflict, apparently led to alcoholism (nonsignificant).

3. Children reared in families characterized by incest or illegitimacy were significantly more likely to become alcoholics in adulthood ($P < .005$).

4. Strongly Catholic mothers produced fewer alcoholic sons than mothers who were weakly Catholic ($P < .02$).

Fifty-five per cent of the alcoholics (as compared to 36 per cent of the nondeviants) had backgrounds of extreme parental conflict, definite neurological disorder, or sexual deviance in the family. Only 7 per cent of the alcoholics (as compared to 25 per cent of the nondeviants) had devoutly Catholic mothers.

4

DEPENDENCY CONFLICT

In the preceding chapters we have indicated that alcoholism was more prevalent in certain ethnic groups than in others, that it was more common among nominally religious people, and that it was more a middle-class than a lower-class phenomenon. In addition, the evidence leads to the conclusion that conflict within a child's family, neural disorder, familial sexual deviance, and parental disagreement over the use of alcohol were often associated with alcoholism. These findings indicate that alcoholism is a response to "stress" or "anxiety" (neurologically or environmentally produced) and that it is aggravated by lax or inconsistent social control over the uses of liquor. Let us now proceed to examine the specific forms of anxiety which promote this particular kind of deviance.

Everyone who has taken a drink knows that alcohol reduces anxiety, tensions, or stress. The person ill-at-ease at a party, or facing an important crisis, or recovering from an emotional shock can find temporary solace in alcohol. Not everyone who uses alcohol to reduce stress proceeds to the eventual state of addiction; some people can take liquor for its relaxing qualities but can still drink with discretion.

What kind of anxiety is so overpowering that it causes the person to become alcoholic? We believe that anxiety which results from an internal conflict between a strong "dependency" need and an equally strong desire for independence is one basic source of the disorder. In this chapter, we present evidence indicating that the alcoholic, in childhood, is subjected to various environmental conditions that contribute to this particular conflict.

By "dependent desires," we mean those urges almost everyone feels at some time in his life to give himself over to unquestioning, undemanding maternal care, to be comforted, and to be guided by someone else. We regard such a dependency "need" as virtually universal. With the exception of the supposedly "feral" men, all human beings undergo a process of socialization, which establishes dependent urges as one of the primary "needs." We would follow such writers as Talcott Parsons, Ian Suttie, and Abraham Maslow in assuming that the infant, after associating the alleviation of hunger pangs with the presence of his mother, comes to value maternal comfort in and for itself. The absence of the mother or rejection by the mother thus becomes an inherently frustrating experience for the child.

We further assume that later experiences in childhood can serve to modify the child's dependent desires in one of three ways. (1) If the desires are consistently satisfied, the need will diminish in intensity and will cease to be a dominating motive. (2) If the desires are consistently frustrated, the dependent motives will tend to be extinguished. (3) If a child's desires are erratically satisfied and frustrated, they should increase in intensity and should, indeed, become one of the most powerful motivating forces in his life.

In American society, everyone in childhood finds himself in a more or less dependent position. As age advances, however, society imposes demands on the individual to give up his dependent state and to accept the independence required in adult life. Males in American society are especially subject to a cultural proscription that dependent desires and behavior should be relinquished. The male role is defined as involving independence, strength, courage, and resoluteness. These qualities are incompatible with desires to be "cared-for" and "mothered." Thus, for American men, the switch from childhood dependency to adult independence is uniquely severe.

Our belief is that certain men, including potential alcoholics, undergo early experiences that heighten their dependent desires and, at the same time, create uncertainty about the kind of behavior that will satisfy their urges. One alternative for people caught in such a conflict—the alternative which the alcoholics seem to choose—is to suppress their dependent desires and to behave in an outwardly independent manner; in other words, to deny totally any form of dependent behavior.

We would argue that parents alternating between lavish satisfaction of the child's dependent desires and subsequent punishment of these same urges would create in the boy a heightened desire for maternal care. Conflict is created within him: his desires are satisfied, he is given a taste of pleasure—then the satisfactions are whipped away by a change in the parents' mood. Because of the parents' behavior, the child does not know how to satisfy his dependent needs.

When such a boy grows up, he may find the usual male role markedly distasteful. His heightened urges for maternal care cannot be legitimately satisfied in the normal performance of an adult male role.

Liquor provides a suitable outlet for the person plagued by such a dependency conflict. Drinking in American society is, typically, a "masculine" act: it conforms with the male role. At the same time, under the influence of heavy doses of liquor, a person can feel "cared for" and comforted; his troubles flee, his desire for dependency is satisfied. Heavy drinking removes the conflict between dependency desires and the necessities of the male role.

Our opinion concerning the nature of alcoholic tendencies derived from an examination of the early conditions of the alcoholic's life. In this chapter, therefore, we offer several pieces of evidence that appear to support the hypothesis.

THE MOTHER'S ATTITUDE TOWARD THE CHILD

In American society, a child is dependent on his mother for a relatively long period. During this time, some of the child's most basic tendencies are established. One of the more important of these fundamental attitudes is the child's dependency longings. To see what relation maternal attitudes toward the child bore to adult alcoholism, we categorized the mothers and then related maternal attitudes to the sons' alcoholic tendencies.

The largest number of mothers could be regarded as *actively affectionate.* They welcomed the child's presence (at least most of the time), enjoyed him as a person, talked with pride about his character and activities, and showed, in other ways, their affectionate regard for him.

Other mothers could be regarded as *passively affectionate.* They seldom gave evidence of their affection in an outwardly demonstrative fashion; nevertheless, their attitudes were generally approving, or at least they expressed concern for the child.

Twenty-four mothers were rated as *rejecting.* They volunteered statements like, "I wish that kid had never been born," or, "He's a pain in the neck. I wish I could get rid of him." They cared little about the child's health or well-being. The majority of these women expressed their rejection by neglect or avoidance; nine of the rejecting mothers were overtly cruel in their treatment of the child.

A final group of mothers erratically varied between being affectionate with their children and rejecting them. An *alternating* mother would, at times, smother her child with kisses, compliment him extravagantly, take care of his needs with great concern, and speak of him with pride. At other times, however, she responded with extreme rejection, neglect, denial of his worth, and other evidences of profound dislike.

Mothers who alternated between affection and rejection produced the highest proportion of alcoholic sons, and actively affectionate mothers produced the lowest proportion of alcoholic sons ($P < .005$):[1]

MOTHER'S ATTITUDE TOWARD THE BOY
AND ALCOHOLISM

	Per Cent Who Became Alcoholics
Actively affectionate mother (N: 99)	8
Passively affectionate mother (N: 37)	19
Rejecting mother (N: 24)	21
Alternating mother (N: 23)	35

We assumed that the behavior of alternating mothers—encouraging, but also punishing, the child's desire for maternal care—created a basic conflict in the child. While desire for maternal care would be sporadically rewarded, satisfaction would be irregular. (It should be noted that sporadic gratification of hunger tends to increase the desire for food.) It seems reasonable to postulate that the sons raised by alternating mothers were filled with anxiety about their desire for maternal care. Their wish to be dependent was tantalized by the alternation of reward and punishment. Experience with their mothers taught them that their status was insecure, thereby creating more anxiety about how to achieve the reward of maternal care.

The rejecting and the passive mothers, by consistently denying the boy's dependent longings, would have a tendency to extinguish dependent behavior. The actively affectionate mothers, on the other hand, would consistently satisfy their sons' dependency urges and therefore would produce little conflict over dependency.

What occurred when maternal erraticism was combined with generalized conflict between the parents? We found previously that familial conflict increased the son's chances of alcoholism (presumably because such conflict created greater internal stress within the child). As the table shows, a child raised in an antagonistic environment by an alternating, passive, or rejecting mother had the greatest tendency to become alcoholic, and one raised in a home with little conflict by an actively affectionate mother had the least tendency to become alcoholic (P < .001).[2]

PARENTAL CONFLICT, MATERNAL ATTITUDES,
AND ALCOHOLISM
(*Per Cent Who Became Alcoholics*)

Maternal Attitude	Parental Conflict			
	Little		Intense	
Actively affectionate	(N: 61)	5	(N: 23)	13
Passively affectionate	(N: 21)	10	(N: 10)	30
Rejecting	(N: 13)	15	(N: 7)	29
Alternating	(N: 13)	23	(N: 8)	50

Both the parental conflict and the maternal relation to the child apparently influenced the rate of alcoholism and were not simply reflections of the other. Whether there was "little" or "intense" conflict, alternating mothers produced the highest proportion of alcoholic sons. Parental conflict seemed to increase alcoholism rates regardless of the mothers' attitudes toward their sons.

Thus, it would seem that parental conflict produced in the child a general instability that tended to be channeled into adult alcoholism when the mother created a dependency conflict in her son. In other words, a child raised in an environment embittered by both parental conflict and absence of maternal affection had about seven times the chance of becoming an alcoholic as a boy reared by an affectionate mother in a home where there was little conflict.

THE MOTHER'S ATTITUDE TOWARD SOCIETY

A child is influenced not only by his mother's attitude toward him but also by other important aspects of her behavior. He perceives her reaction to crises and her attitudes toward people outside the family and toward the moral precepts of society. These factors, we found, were related to whether or not her son became alcoholic when he reached adulthood.

The Mother's Reaction to Crises

When faced with an important emotional problem, does the mother meet it realistically, in a fashion that may resolve the issue, or does she choose some unrealistic path? Certainly her behavior in a crucial situation will affect her son's regard for her, his trust in her judgment, and his feeling of security.

In order to investigate the relation between alcoholism and the mother's outward behavior, we categorized each mother according to the way she commonly faced crises. The pressures created by the depression and the Second World War supplied many opportunities to observe the mother's reactions. The staff could watch her handle such problems as unemployment, erratic behavior by the father (desertion of the family, alcoholism, brutality), family arguments, severe disagreement between the children and their parents, and other crises typical of family life in an urban area. A number of women could not be categorized; either their reactions to crises varied too greatly or the observers were not present when the crises occurred. Other mothers, however, gave evidence of a consistent pattern; when faced with an important issue, they regularly reacted in a similar fashion.

The largest group of mothers realistically faced the problem. Whatever the issue, the action they chose was calculated to ameliorate the situation in a relatively rational way.

Twenty-two mothers consistently reacted to crises with aggression. Regardless of the causes or the consequences, these women attacked whatever frustrated them.

Another set of mothers withdrew from crises. When faced with an issue, they evaded the situation. Commonly, they changed the subject, retired to their rooms, or ignored the situation. Five women, however, became promiscuous at times of crises (four of their sons became alcoholics) and two began to drink (neither of their sons became alcoholic). These various types of reactions were considered as escapist.

We found relatively little alcoholism among the sons of women who faced crises realistically or who responded aggressively to such situations; a higher proportion of those whose mothers escaped from crises had become alcoholics (P < .02).[3]

MOTHER'S REACTION TO CRISES AND ALCOHOLISM

	Per Cent Who Became Alcoholics
Faced realistically (N: 105)	15
Attacked (N: 22)	14
Escaped (N: 24)	38

One could hypothesize that the mother's escapism increased the child's dependency conflict by making him unsure whether she would protect and comfort him in a crisis.

The Mother's Deviant Behavior

Certain kinds of behavior are judged as "deviant" by the dominant standards of society. In the northern urban area where the study was conducted, three types of behavior were (at least, verbally) condemned: female alcoholism, sexual infidelity, and overt criminality.

From extended observation of the mother's behavior (and from court and social agency records) judgments could be made concerning these forms of deviance. The large majority of women in the study could be considered as *nondeviant.* Seven mothers had been convicted for criminal acts; fourteen were quite regularly sexually unfaithful to their husbands; and fifteen were or had been chronic alcoholics. These women composed a blatantly deviant group.

As one might expect, the deviant mothers produced a significantly greater number of alcoholic sons (P < .02).[4]

MATERNAL DEVIANCE AND ALCOHOLISM

	Per Cent Who Became Alcoholics
Alcoholic mother (N: 15)	33
Deviant, nonalcoholic, mother (N: 12)	33
Nondeviant mother (N: 157)	13

The particular form of deviance in which the mother participated did not make a difference. Criminally or sexually deviant mothers produced as high a proportion of alcoholic sons as did the chronic alcoholic mothers. These facts seem to indicate that the sons were not simply imitating their mothers' alcoholism, but that any type of major deviation by the mother tended to result in high alcoholism rates. This tendency remained when we held constant two other conditions that were significantly related to alcoholism: (1) an absence of maternal love and (2) parental conflict.

Regardless of the mother's emotional attitude toward the child, her deviant behavior tended to produce addiction in her son:

MATERNAL ATTITUDE, MATERNAL DEVIANCE, AND ALCOHOLISM
(Per Cent Who Became Alcoholics)

Maternal Attitude	Maternal Deviance			
	Deviant		Nondeviant	
Actively affectionate	(N: 10)	20	(N: 89)	8
Passively affectionate	(N: 4)	25	(N: 32)	19
Rejecting	(N: 5)	40	(N: 19)	16
Alternating	(N: 7)	57	(N: 16)	25

It seems that both the mother's emotional attitude and her behavior had some influence in causing alcoholism. Deviant mothers produced higher rates of alcoholism among their sons, whether they were affectionate or unaffectionate. (Maternal deviance seems to have been most conducive to alcoholism when the mother was not affectionate.) Among nondeviant mothers, a lack of consistent maternal affection tended to produce more alcoholics $(P < .02)$.[5]

A lack of affection seems to have led most directly to alcoholism when it was combined with maternal deviance. A combination of deviance with a lack of affection resulted in a 50 per cent alcoholism rate; only deviance or only absence of active maternal affection resulted in a 20 per cent alcoholism rate; sons of actively affectionate, nondeviant women had an 8 per cent alcoholism rate $(P < .001)$.[6]

In dissecting the effects of parental conflict and maternal deviance, one finds that maternal deviance had a more pronounced effect when there was also parental conflict. The highest rate of alcoholism was found in the families that were disrupted by conflict and maternal deviance $(P < .001)$.[7]

MATERNAL DEVIANCE, PARENTAL CONFLICT,
AND ALCOHOLISM
(*Per Cent Who Became Alcoholics*)

Parental Conflict	Maternal Behavior			
	Deviant		Nondeviant	
Little	(N: 7)	0	(N: 100)	11
Intense	(N: 15)	47	(N: 33)	15

Alcoholism rates among sons of nondeviant women barely reflected the amount of family conflict. Among sons of deviants, parental conflict did seem to aggravate alcoholism-producing forces (nonsignificant).

On the other hand, maternal deviance resulted in significantly more alcoholism among families irritated by intense conflict $(P < .05)$.[8]

By holding constant the other influential factors of maternal attitude toward the child and the degree of parental conflict, the analyses reveal that maternal deviance tended to create more alcoholic sons. Since the child did not appear to be merely imitating his alcoholic mother, it seems reasonable to assume that maternal deviance led to a conflict in satisfying his dependent urges. Deviant behavior presumably conflicted with the opinions of other people who influenced the child. One can reasonably assume that a child raised by such a mother lost respect for her, while at the same time, his desire to be loved by her continued; a conflict would be established between his desire for care and his desire to deny dependence on an unreliable maternal figure.

In summary, the mothers of alcoholics tended to have reacted unrealistically by withdrawal when faced with crises and to have themselves deviated from societal norms in their behavior. Each of these patterns, we believe, would tend to undermine a child's confidence in his mother. Within the family, too, we found that variables dealing with the mother's status were related to alcoholism.

THE MOTHER IN RELATION TO HER FAMILY

Three additional measures of the emotional tone in the family were associated with adult alcoholism: the father's esteem for his wife, the nature of the affectional relationship between the parents, and the acceptance or resentment shown by the mother of her role in the family.

The Father's Esteem for His Wife

From the father's point of view, we had a measure of the mother's status in the family. The greatest number of fathers either moderately or highly esteemed their wives. They openly commented on their wives' ability, complimented them for their achievements, and spoke with gratitude about them; some simply accepted their wives without overt signs of either approval or disapproval. Other fathers, however, undermined the mother's importance, described her activities with sarcasm, and openly spoke of her faults.

Fathers who showed little esteem for their wives had a significantly higher rate of alcoholism among their sons $(P < .005)$.[9]

THE FATHER'S ESTEEM FOR HIS WIFE
AND ALCOHOLISM

Per Cent Who Became Alcoholics

Moderate or high (N: 100) 11
Low (N: 38) 32

In line with our previous interpertations, we believe that a conflict would be instilled in the child between his natural wish for maternal care and a repression of his urge, created by the father's persistent description of the mother as "worthless."

As one would expect, the children raised by a deviant mother *and* a father who undermined the status of the mother had the highest rate of alcoholism (P < .005).[10]

MATERNAL DEVIANCE, FATHER'S ESTEEM FOR MOTHER,
AND ALCOHOLISM
(*Per Cent Who Became Alcoholics*)

Father's Esteem for Mother	Maternal Deviance			
	Deviant		Nondeviant	
Moderate or high	(N: 12)	8	(N: 86)	12
Low	(N: 11)	55	(N: 27)	22

It is interesting to note that if the father regarded the mother with relatively high esteem, the mother's deviant behavior was not reflected in the son's alcoholism.

The father's low esteem for his wife and her rejection of her son were highly correlated. We therefore sought to check whether the apparent influence of each on alcoholism would remain when we held the other constant. The results of this analysis can be seen in the following:

FATHER'S ESTEEM FOR THE MOTHER, MATERNAL ATTITUDE
TOWARD THE CHILD, AND ALCOHOLISM
(*Per Cent Who Became Alcoholics*)

Mother's Attitude	Father's Esteem for Mother			
	High		Low	
Actively affectionate	(N: 53)	8	(N: 15)	13
Passively affectionate	(N: 22)	9	(N: 7)	57
Rejecting	(N: 10)	10	(N: 7)	29
Alternating	(N: 12)	25	(N: 9)	44

Among boys whose fathers had low esteem for their wives, those whose mothers were either passive or who alternated between affection and rejection had a significantly higher rate of alcoholism (P < .05).[11] The absence of active maternal affection together with low paternal esteem for the mother led to increased alcoholism: 43 per cent of those whose fathers had low esteem for their wives, as compared to 14 per cent of those whose fathers had high esteem for their wives, became alcoholics (P < .01).[12]

Thus, this evidence suggests that both maternal rejection of the son and paternal denigration of the mother can heighten the son's addictive propensities.

Affectional Attitudes Between the Parents

The amount of affection displayed by one parent for the other seemed also to be related to alcoholism. In rating the affectional relation between the parents, three categories were used:

The majority of the families could be considered as *affectionate*; the parents generally had a high regard for each other's welfare (regardless of the presence or absence of conflict). At the minimum, concern was displayed in times of illness or on other sporadic occasions. Parents in the second group were overtly *antagonistic*. They constantly battled in the home and they seemed to take pleasure in discomfiting one another. A small number of families were *indifferent*; the parents led their own lives, paying little attention to each other. Their lack of contact may have emerged from hostile attitudes, but hostility was not expressed openly; essentially, the relationship could be considered "cold."

The openly hostile, antagonistic parents produced the highest proportion of alcoholic sons (P < .02).[13]

PARENTAL AFFECTION AND ALCOHOLISM

	Per Cent Who Became Alcoholics
Affectionate parents (N: 93)	13
Indifferent parents (N: 14)	7
Antagonistic parents (N: 37)	30

One can argue that parental antagonism would be another influence leading to dependency conflict. The child, torn between two antagonistic parents, would find it difficult to feel secure with either.

The Mother's Role in the Family

A small proportion of the mothers in the study clearly dominated family affairs without consultation or consideration of others' opinions; these were designated as *dictators*. The majority of mothers actively participated in family decisions; these were called *leaders*. A third group of mothers made almost no decisions within the family; their role was considered as *passive*. These three types of mothers had clearly defined roles. A very small group of mothers were found to be resentful of their roles. Some of them played the role of *martyr*; these women were both passive (in that they refused to make decisions) and dominating (in that they refused to accept decisions made by others), showing clear evidence of a deep resentment of their position in the home. The remainder of the mothers whose role was ambiguous neither led nor followed; there was no clear evidence, however, that they viewed themselves as martyrs for they participated very little in family affairs; these *neglecting* women attempted to dissociate themselves from the other members of the family.

Alcoholism rates were significantly higher among the sons of women who resented their role in the family (P < .005).[14]

The Mother's Role in the Family and Alcoholism

	Per Cent Who Became Alcoholics
Dictator (N: 9)	11
Leader (N: 124)	13
Passive (N: 30)	13
Martyr (N: 10)	40
Neglecting (N: 8)	50

We have demonstrated that alcoholism was related to three dimensions of the mother's position in the family: her status in the eyes of her husband, the nature of her emotional interaction with her husband, and resentment of her role in the family. Low status, parental antagonism, and the mother's resentment of her family role, we believe, would tend to give rise to dependency conflict in the child.

SOME NEGATIVE FINDINGS

As we noted earlier, sexual explanations for alcoholism have received some prominence. Yet this research offers little support for the specifically sexual explanations of the disorder. We have already pointed out that in our sample, boys characterized by obvious oral tendencies or by latently homosexual behavior did not become alcoholic significantly more often than those without these traits. Nevertheless, the significant associations reported in this chapter, particularly those concerned with the mother's emotional relationship with the child, could easily be subsumed under a psychoanalytic explanation of the disorder. To discover whether such an interpretation would aid in understanding the alcoholic, we further investigated the degree to which specifically sexual factors were related to the genesis of alcoholism.

One such factor was the degree of sexual anxiety exhibited by a child's mother. A mother bothered by intense sexual anxiety could well transmit this anxiety to her children. Consequently, we examined the degree to which sex anxiety in the mother affected the rate of adult alcoholism in the sons.

Most of the mothers in the study had no more than the usual amount of sexual anxiety; they adhered to certain taboos, felt rather stringent inhibitions of their sexual drives, and seldom discussed the subject. Nevertheless, their relations with their husbands were presumably satisfactory; they could talk to their children about sex without undue anxiety; and they did not exhibit an *overt* concern (positive or negative) with sexual matters.

Nineteen mothers, on the other hand, evidenced intense sexual anxiety. They could not give their children sexual information or handle normal relationships with their husbands. They often expressed their disgust with sex and found it extremely difficult to picture sexual relations as other than "dirty."

Thirty-eight mothers fell between these two extremes. At times, they appeared to have intense feelings of anxiety; while at other times, they could face sexual matters with relative freedom.

We assumed that if sexual anxiety in the parents was related to the son's alcoholism, those mothers who evinced the most intense anxiety would produce more alcoholic sons. Although the tendency was as predicted, the difference was slight.

MOTHER'S SEXUAL ANXIETY AND ALCOHOLISM

	Per Cent Who Became Alcoholics
Little sexual anxiety (N: 90)	16
Some sexual anxiety (N: 38)	16
Intense sexual anxiety (N: 19)	21

68 DEPENDENCY CONFLICT

Mothers who had intense sexual anxiety did not create a significantly greater proportion of alcoholic sons; this part of the mother's character apparently has much less relevance than her emotional attitude toward the child, her reaction to crises, or her perception of her role.

A different aspect of the mother's behavior—whether or not she had shifted husbands—might, we thought, influence alcoholism. In the context of Freudian theory, it seems reasonable to presume that mothers who had more than one husband might produce sexual jealousy and frustration in their sons and, hence, lead their sons toward alcoholism. This assumption, too, proved incorrect.

FREQUENCY OF MOTHER'S MARRIAGES AND ALCOHOLISM

	Per Cent Who Became Alcoholics
One marriage (N: 164)	16
More than one marriage (N: 22)	14

Mothers who had married more than once did not have a greater tendency to produce alcoholic sons than did mothers who had married only once.

In addition to these fairly direct measures designed to tap the role of sex anxiety in the production of alcoholism, we rated the mothers on two scales designed to indicate how she might indirectly promote anxiety in the boy concerning his masculinity: her encouragement of dependent behavior and her encouragement of "masculine" activities.

We assumed that the mother's encouragement of dependency (i.e., rewarding her child when he behaved in a dependent fashion) would tend to make her child more dependent on her. We rated such behavior on a two-point scale. If alcoholics simply had a greater desire for dependent relationships (rather than a conflict over dependency), we reasoned, strong maternal encouragement of dependency should lead to high alcoholism rates.* This did not prove to be the case:

* This scale had a significant negative relation to criminal rates (X^2 4.2; d.f. 1), a fact which tends to indicate its validity.

MOTHER'S ENCOURAGEMENT OF DEPENDENCY
AND ALCOHOLISM

Per Cent Who Became Alcoholics

Strong (N: 70) 13
Moderate or weak (N: 104) 19

Using a different approach, we sought to discover the relationship to alcoholism of the mother's encouragement or discouragement of such "masculine" activities as playing ball, watching football games, fishing. Discouragement of masculine behavior, we assumed, might lead to latent homosexual tendencies (urges that might not be directly shown in the child's behavior as this was defined for our rating of the boys). Using a three-point scale, we found that alcoholism rates were approximately equal for each group:

MOTHER'S ENCOURAGEMENT OF MASCULINITY
AND ALCOHOLISM

Per Cent Who Became Alcoholics

Strongly encouraged (N: 20) 15
Moderately encouraged (N: 118) 16
Discouraged (N: 26) 15

Thus, we found no relationship between alcoholism and the mother's encouragement of dependency, her discouragement of masculine activities, the frequency of the mother's marriages, or the intensity of her sexual anxiety. It would appear, therefore, that sexual confusion or anxiety in the child's background did not play an important part in promoting alcoholism.

SUMMARY: DEPENDENCY CONFLICT AS A SOURCE OF ALCOHOLISM

We have argued throughout this chapter that the anxiety generated by an intense dependency conflict produces alcoholism. By dependency conflict, we mean the clash between a desire for maternal care (made more intense than usual because of erratic variation between frustration and satisfaction) and an equally strong desire for independence.

Almost every male in American society has a more or less

vague self-image of independence, courage, dependability, and resoluteness instilled in him through his culture. Every male in America is expected, to some extent, to give up dependent desires. In the potential alcoholic, we have argued, this sacrifice is particularly difficult for two reasons: first, his treatment as a child has led to heightened dependency desires; second, his background has given him reason to believe that dependency is either impossible, undesirable, or immoral. The normal requirements of the male role in America put even more pressure on the potential alcoholic to deny his dependent urges.

A person with dependency conflict may resolve the dilemma in a variety of ways. He may attempt to repress his desire for maternal care and take out his resulting frustration in certain psychosomatic illnesses, e.g., ulcers.* He may, on the other hand, arrange his life in such a fashion that one of his conflicting desires is fully satisfied—he might, for example, marry a dominating, loving woman and secure satisfaction of his dependency urges. Similarly, he might become a hobo and reject entirely the cultural demands for independence and responsibility. He might, on the other hand, withdraw completely from the world by joining an institution, such as the professional army or a monastic order, thus maintaining a semblance of masculinity and simultaneously satisfying his need to be "mothered" by others in authority.

Thus, alcoholism is by no means an inevitable solution to the conflict. In current American society, it is, nevertheless, a relatively appealing alternative in that it satisfies the man's dependent needs and allows him to maintain an independent, masculine self-image.

This interpretation of alcoholism is speculative—as all theories of human nature, in this stage, must be. It is obviously based on assumptions concerning the existence of a dependency need and the relation between early experiences and the intensity of this desire. We believe, however, that the evidence reported in this study tends to support the theory.

---

* Although there has been no longitudinal analysis of the problem, we would hypothesize that the genesis of alcoholism closely resembles the origins of such psychogenic diseases as ulcers, migraine headaches, arthritis, and hypochondria. All these disorders appear to have a common element: they could serve to reduce dependency conflict.

In Chapter 8, which outlines the personality of the pre-alcoholics, we will demonstrate that the pre-alcoholics as children behaved in ways which could be interpreted as extreme denial of dependent desires. In this chapter, we have shown that children who undergo several kinds of experiences that would be expected to increase dependency conflict tend to become alcoholics as adults.

Specifically, we have shown that the following early influences bear a significantly positive relation to adult alcoholism:

1. Maternal alternation between active affection and rejection ($P < .02$);

2. Maternal escapism ($P < .02$);

3. Deviant—i.e., criminal, promiscuous, or alcoholic—behavior of the mother ($P < .02$);

4. Denigration of the mother by the father ($P < .005$);

5. Antagonistic relationship between the parents ($P < .02$);

6. Maternal resentment of her role in the family ($P < .005$);

Seventy-three per cent of the alcoholics had family backgrounds characterized by at least one of these six types of behavior.

On the other hand, we have shown that certain other measures pertaining to the mother are not related to adult alcoholism: maternal passivity, the mother's sex anxiety, the number of husbands the mother has had, her encouragement of dependency in her son, and her discouragement of masculine behavior on the son's part.

Naturally, many of these measures were correlated with one another. Hampered by the small size of the sample, we nevertheless held constant some of the factors that might have falsely pointed to a connection between a single measure and adult alcoholism. By this process, we have shown that absence of active maternal affection, maternal deviance, and denigration of the mother by the father resulted in higher alcoholism rates even when other conditions were held constant. The relationship between these dependency factors and backgrounds of family conflict, sex deviance, and neural disorder was strong. Nevertheless, alcoholism rates reflected the number of dependency variables when "stress" was held constant. The cumulative influence on alcoholism rates of the six dependency variables gives further indication that alcoholism is at least partially a response to conflict over dependency in childhood.

NUMBER OF DEPENDENCY CONFLICT VARIABLES, STRESS,[a]
AND ALCOHOLISM
(*Per Cent Who Became Alcoholics*)

Dependency Factors	Stress		No Stress		Total	
None	(N: 17)	0	(N: 86)	10	(N: 103)	9
One	(N: 17)	12	(N: 21)	10	(N: 38)	11
Two	(N: 18)	22	(N: 7)	14	(N: 25)	20
Three to six .	(N: 19)	52	(N: 2)	50	(N: 21)	52

[a] Family conflict, neural disorder, or sexual deviance in family constituted the "stress" variables. Maternal alternation, escapism, deviance, role resentment; parental antagonism; and paternal denigration of the mother were the "dependency conflict" factors.

In attempting to bring meaning to these various results, we have made interpretations that are not fully supported by the evidence. We have no direct evidence, for example, that ambivalent treatment causes dependency conflict. Yet a conflict over dependency desires seems to us to be the most likely result of the treatment the alcoholics received in childhood.

5

ROLE CONFUSION

We have argued that dependency conflict is a primary source of alcoholism; but we must also recognize that the anxiety bred by such a conflict can be resolved in a number of ways. Thus, the question remains: Why does a person, caught in a dependency conflict, choose alcohol addiction? A major part of the answer, we believe, can be found by examining the childhood experiences that prepare a boy for his role as an adult.

A child normally develops his self-expectations as a result of the expectations others have of him or through observation of his male model, his father. This chapter puts forth the argument that alcoholics have a confused image of the male role, that they are not trained, either by example or by discipline, to accept responsibilities. The evidence indicates that a confused perception of role expectations, an inadequate self-image, is highly productive of alcoholism.

Before proceeding with this analysis, it should be noted that we did not possess information on the boys' actual self-images. Consequently, in this chapter, we examine the boys' environments and propose some hypotheses concerning the presumed effect of these experiences on the subjects' self-concepts. In effect, we are utilizing the idea of a confused self-image as an intervening variable, which we believe can explain the association between the boys' backgrounds and their eventual alcoholism.

Two early conditions, we believe, have led to inadequate role perception: first, there seems to have been reason for the alcoholics to reject the masculine role represented by their fathers; second, the alcoholic seems to have received little guidance in the acceptance of responsibility. Both of these conditions, we hypothesize, would lead to a confused perception of the male role. Basically confused in his self-image, such a person could take refuge from responsibility through alcoholism.

THE PATERNAL MODEL

In the preceding chapter, we indicated the fundamental importance of the mother-son relationship to adult alcoholism, finding that overt maternal ambivalence was strongly productive of adult alcoholism. The attitudes of the boys' fathers toward them had been categorized on the same scale, ranging from actively affectionate to actively rejecting. The relationship between the father's attitude toward his son and alcoholism can be seen in the following table:

PATERNAL ATTITUDE TOWARD THE CHILD AND ALCOHOLISM

	Per Cent Who Became Alcoholics
Actively affectionate father (N: 55)	11
Passively affectionate father (N: 47)	15
Alternating father (N: 14)	14
Passively rejecting father (N: 19)	16
Actively rejecting father (N: 20)	30

Only active paternal rejection seemed to result in high alcoholism rates. This finding was the first to suggest that the son's rejection of the father may play some part in producing alcoholism.

On the basis of this suggestion, we hypothesized that a father who had dominant control of his son (who was the son's primary disciplinarian) and who exerted control physically—by spankings, beatings, or harsh verbal abuse—would also tend to be rejected by his son.

We had recorded the major disciplinary agent of each subject. A majority, of course, were disciplined primarily by their mothers. Yet sixty-one boys were disciplined primarily by their fathers. (A small minority received their discipline from someone other than their parents.) In addition to recording the major disciplining agent, we categorized the techniques of discipline used. We considered as "punitive discipline" those methods which depended upon physical force for their effectiveness (e.g., beatings, spankings, and extremely harsh verbal abuse). Other techniques (scolding, isolation, removal of privileges) were considered as "nonpunitive."

By combining these two factors, we were able to compare the effects on alcoholism rates of the father's techniques of discipline when he was and when he was not the primary disciplinarian.

FATHER'S DISCIPLINARY TECHNIQUE, MAJOR DISCIPLINARIAN, AND ALCOHOLISM
(*Per Cent Who Became Alcoholics*)

Father's Discipline	Major Disciplinary Agent			
	Father		Not Father	
Punitive	(N: 47)	23	(N: 37)	11
Nonpunitive	(N: 16)	0	(N: 47)	17

Thus again, we found a (nonsignificant) tendency toward alcoholism under conditions that might be expected to lead to the son's rejection of his father. It should be noted that among the boys whose mothers were their primary disciplinarians, 12 per cent of those who received punitive discipline as compared to 18 per cent of those who received nonpunitive discipline had become alcoholics. Therefore punitiveness as such was not related to high alcoholism.

Both overt paternal rejection and paternal punitiveness seemed to lead to alcoholism; yet the numbers were few and neither relationship was found to be statistically significant. When, however, we computed alcoholism rates for the forty-four fathers who were *either* overtly rejecting, or punitive and not actively affectionate, we found that 27 per cent of their sons had become alcoholics, whereas only 12 per cent of the sons of neither rejecting nor punitive fathers had become alcoholics (P < .02).[1]

Paternal antagonism (overt rejection or controlling punitiveness) resulted in high rates of alcoholism. We believe that this effect is due to the fact that a boy would tend to reject an antagonistic father as a model. Other conditions, of course, might lead to rejection of the paternal model—or, conversely, paternal antagonism may lead to alcoholism for some reason other than the one we propose.

We rejected the hypothesis that paternal antagonism leads to heightened aggression directed against the self, thereby leading to alcoholism, because none of the other measures of aggression (see Chapter 7) were related to alcoholism.

One alternative hypothesis we had entertained centered around identification with an escapist father. We had recorded the father's reaction to various types of crises and, as we did for the mother's, had divided them into three relatively distinct groupings: those who attempted to find some realistic solution to the problem; those who reacted with aggression, regardless of the cause of the crises or the probability that aggression would ameliorate the situation; and those who responded in an escapist fashion through withdrawal from the situation, desertion of the environment, or drinking. Not surprisingly, children whose fathers responded to crises by "escaping" had a significantly higher rate of alcoholism $(P < .025)$.[2]

FATHER'S REACTION TO CRISES AND ALCOHOLISM

	Per Cent Who Became Alcoholics
Realistic reaction to crises (N: 51)	9
Aggressive reaction to crises (N: 18) ...	11
Escapist reaction to crises (N: 56)	25

Why did paternal escapism result in high alcoholism rates? We divided the escapist and the nonescapist fathers into groups according to their affection for their sons. We assumed that if the relationship between paternal escapism and alcoholism was due to identification (and if the identification occurs in response to affection), then alcoholism rates should be highest when the escapist father had been affectionate. This was not the case.

PATERNAL REACTION TO CRISES, PATERNAL ATTITUDE TOWARD THE CHILD, AND ALCOHOLISM
(Per Cent Who Became Alcoholics)

Reaction to Crises	Affectionate Fathers		Alternating or Rejecting Fathers	
Escapist	(N: 23)	26	(N: 28)	25
Aggressive or realistic	(N: 50)	10	(N: 13)	8

Since the theory of identification seemed to receive little support from our material,* we hypothesized that a father who escaped from crises—because he fails to fulfill his son's role expectations for him—tends to be rejected by his son. This reasoning depends upon our belief that children exposed to general cultural stereotypes come to expect their parents to play certain roles, to behave in certain ways. For the father, this would involve (among other things) the ability to meet crises with courage—for "courage" is one of the cornerstones of the stereotype "manliness." We related paternal escapism to alcoholism, therefore, because it tended to result in the boy's rejection of his male model.

Although we were unable to check this hypothesis directly, it seemed to account for the relationship between alcoholism and paternal antagonism (i.e., overt rejection by the father or his controlling punitiveness) and escapism. This relationship is shown in the following chart:

PATERNAL ESCAPISM, PATERNAL ANTAGONISM, AND ALCOHOLISM
(*Per Cent Who Became Alcoholics*)

	Father Antagonistic		Father Not Antagonistic	
Father escapist	(N: 17)	35	(N: 36)	22
Father not escapist	(N: 29)	21	(N: 105)	9

The highest alcoholism rate appeared when paternal antagonism was combined with paternal escapism, and the lowest rate occurred in the absence of both $(P < .005)$.[3] The rates were almost identical if the father was antagonistic but not escapist, and vice versa. In other words, alcoholism rates were highest under circumstances which would be likely to lead to rejection of the paternal model: when the father was either overtly rejecting or strongly punitive and also escaped when faced with crises. It seems reasonable to presume that sons will reject antagonistic fathers or fathers who fail to fulfill their sons' expectations concerning the paternal role.

* See below and also Chapters 2 and 7.

From the reports of various observers, court records, and social agency information, we had discovered that fifty-one of the fathers were alcoholics. An additional twenty-three fathers (nonalcoholic) were either criminal or blatantly unfaithful to their wives. Unless a father gave evidence of one of these forms of behavior, we considered him a nondeviant. By computing the alcoholism rates among these three groups, we hoped to ascertain the relevance of identification to alcoholism:

PATERNAL DEVIANCE AND ALCOHOLISM

	Per Cent Who Became Alcoholics
Alcoholic father (N: 51)	22
Deviant, nonalcoholic father (N: 23)	17
Nondeviant father (N: 103)	11

Although paternal deviance may lead to alcoholism, the difference was not statistically significant.

Since the affectional relationship between father and son may be assumed to influence the phenomenon of identification, we sought further evidence linking the son's alcoholism to the father's deviance by holding constant the father's attitude toward his child.

FATHER'S ATTITUDE TOWARD THE CHILD, PATERNAL DEVIANCE, AND ALCOHOLISM
(*Per Cent Who Became Alcoholics*)

Father's Attitude	Deviant Father		Nondeviant Father	
Actively affectionate	(N: 12)	17	(N: 41)	10
Passively affectionate	(N: 17)	12	(N: 29)	14
Alternating	(N: 10)	10	(N: 4)	25
Passively rejecting	(N: 9)	33	(N: 10)	0
Actively rejecting	(N: 12)	33	(N: 8)	25

Again, we found no significant relationship between paternal deviance and alcoholism.

As a final test, we thought that perhaps conflict between the parents might tend to reduce identification with the father. Yet when we held constant the degree of parental conflict, we found no reliable relationship between paternal deviance and alcoholism.

PATERNAL DEVIANCE, PARENTAL CONFLICT, AND ALCOHOLISM
(*Per Cent Who Became Alcoholics*)

	Deviant Father		Nondeviant Father	
Intense conflict	(N: 42)	24	(N: 5)	20
Some conflict	(N: 28)	7	(N: 27)	11
Little conflict	(N: 8)	25	(N: 44)	9

Thus, again we failed to find confirmation of the theory which would link alcoholism to paternal deviance through identification.

We have, on the other hand, found some evidence indicating the alcoholic's rejection of the male model: paternal antagonism (either overt rejection or controlling punitiveness) and paternal escapism were significantly related to adult alcoholism.

SPECIFICATION OF ROLE EXPECTATIONS

Observing an acceptable model is one way a child prepares for his role as an adult. Yet parents do not normally rely solely upon the "process of identification" in their attempts to teach the child to accept responsibilities and to control his impulses.

After reading each case record, we noted the types of behavior which the parents expected of the child. We considered only the expectations or demands placed upon the child without considering how they were imposed. Demands were considered "high" if the child was expected to maintain his school work and perform some tasks around the home (e.g., clean his room, prepare meals, do the shopping, care for a younger child), or if demands in either area were very high. Demands were considered "moderate" if the child was expected to perform only small tasks around the home or simply to avoid "trouble" in school. Demands were considered "low" if almost no responsibilities were placed upon the child, that is, if the parents were willing to do the child's school work for him or if they selected the clothes he should wear or if they simply took no interest in his behavior. (One mother whose son was placed in this "low" group went so far as to tie her son's shoes for him.)

As the table below indicates, parents who placed high demands on their children produced significantly fewer alcoholic sons (P < .01).[4]

PARENTAL DEMANDS ON THE CHILD AND ALCOHOLISM

	Per Cent Who Became Alcoholics
High demands (N: 50)	4
Moderate demands (N: 92)	20
Low demands (N: 44)	20

The fact that high demands reduced the likelihood of alcoholism seems to indicate that alcoholics have not been adequately trained to accept responsibilities. Accordingly, we can say that relatively low demands are related to alcoholism.

Expectations for the child may, of course, vary in other ways than degree. Those in charge of the child may themselves disagree over the expectations. We have already seen that parental conflict is related to alcoholism; yet we hesitate to interpret this relationship as being due to confusion in expectations, because it is related to other, nonalcoholic, personality disorders and probably generates tensions far larger in scope than confusion over role expectations.

As a more specific measure of confusion in role, we studied the family structure to ascertain whether some adult other than the parents maintained a significant relationship to the child in terms of imposing demands upon him. Fifty-seven subjects were partially under the direct control of some outsider (usually a grandparent). We divided these according to the comparative expectations of the parents and the outsider. The majority gave general support to the parents' values. A second group was relatively independent of the parents—i.e., areas of control were divided in such a way that the outsider neither came into conflict with nor supported the parents' demands or expectations. A third group of outsiders clearly disagreed with the parents in respect to the demands they placed upon the child. We found that families in which there was some adult outsider who imposed demands counter to those of the parents created a significantly higher proportion of alcoholic sons (P < .005).[5]

SIGNIFICANT ADULT (OTHER THAN PARENTS) EXPECTATIONS AND ALCOHOLISM

	Per Cent Who Became Alcoholics
Apparently no significant outsider (N: 130)	12
Outsider, supports parents (N: 28)	14
Outsider, independent of parents (N: 15)	13
Outsider, opposes parents (N: 14)	50

A conflict in expectations might lead to a confused self-image—one factor in role confusion.

Closely related to the parents' demands on the child was the amount of restrictiveness the child experienced. Because the mother generally is charged with control of her children during childhood (and also because maternal overprotection has been linked with alcoholism), we recorded the degree of restrictiveness which the mother exerted over her son. Some of the mothers were highly restrictive, choosing clothes and friends for their children, not only supervising their play but generally refusing to allow them freedom of choice. Others were "subnormally" restrictive, failing almost completely to direct their children. The subnormally restrictive mothers produced the highest proportion of alcoholic sons (P < .05).[6]

MATERNAL RESTRICTIVENESS OF THE BOY AND ALCOHOLISM

	Per Cent Who Became Alcoholics
Highly restrictive mother (N: 62)	10
Normally restrictive mother (N: 58)	14
Subnormally restrictive mother (N: 59)	24

We also measured, but in a somewhat different fashion, the consistency with which adult values were imposed on the child. We classified the boys according to whether or not *someone* was generally present to supervise their activities. The majority of our subjects were supervised by an adult. A rather sizable minority received supervision sporadically; i.e., some adult took charge of the home either during certain periods of childhood or, for example, on weekends. Finally, a small group of boys were left almost entirely unsupervised in their activities. We found that a lack of supervision tended to result in alcoholism (P < .01).[7]

SUPERVISION OF BOY DURING CHILDHOOD AND ALCOHOLISM

	Per Cent Who Became Alcoholics
Present (N: 114)	11
Sporadic (N: 56)	18
Absent (N: 17)	41

Although we hesitate to suggest that subnormal control by the mother and absence of supervision for the child lead necessarily to role confusion, the fact that both of these conditions are significantly related to alcoholism fits well with the hypothesis that alcoholics have an inadequate perception of the roles that society will impose upon them.

Two additional relationships, reported in previous chapters, seem to us to be consistent with the theory that partially attributes alcoholism to tension produced by role confusion. First, alcoholism occurred significantly less frequently among the sons of immigrants—and immigrant families might be expected to make more explicit their demands upon their sons. Second, alcoholism occurred significantly less frequently among the sons of women who were strong in their Catholic faith. Catholicism, of course, may deter alcoholism for many reasons. Yet we believe that, at least partially, Catholicism tends to prevent alcoholism through its provision of clear role specification.

SUMMARY: INADEQUATE PERCEPTION OF ROLE
AS A SOURCE OF ALCOHOLISM

Our evidence indicates that alcoholics differ from "normal" people in that they found reason to reject their paternal models and had few clearly expressed expectations imposed upon them. Presumably these conditions would lead to a confused or distorted self-image. Specifically, we have shown that the following early conditions are significantly related to adult alcoholism:

1. Overt paternal rejection or paternal punitiveness ($P < .02$);
2. Paternal escapist reactions to crises ($P < .025$);
3. Absence of high parental demands for the child ($P < .01$);
4. The influence of an outsider who is in conflict with the parents over expectations for the child ($P < .005$);
5. Subnormal maternal restrictiveness ($P < .05$);
6. Lack of supervision of the child ($P < .01$).

We have hypothesized that paternal antagonism and escapism tend to lead to rejection of the paternal model; that an outsider whose expectations conflict with the parents' confuses the child; and that high demands, on the contrary, would tend to prepare the child for his adult role. Eighty-three per cent of the alcoholics had backgrounds which combined paternal antagonism or escapism or a "conflicting outsider" with an absence of high demands.

A background of parental conflict, neural disorder, or sexual deviance in the family seemed to raise the probability of alcoholism $(P < .05)$.[8] Role confusion resulted in significantly higher alcoholism rates, however, in the absence of these "stress" conditions $(P < .005)$[9] as well as in their presence $(P < .001)$:[10]

ROLE CONFUSION,[a] STRESS,[b] AND ALCOHOLISM
(*Per Cent Who Became Alcoholics*)

Role Confusion	No Stress		Stress	
Absent	(N: 84)	4	(N: 31)	3
Present	(N: 32)	28	(N: 40)	38

[a] Low demands and paternal antagonism or escapism or "conflicting outsider."

[b] Parental conflict, neural disorder, or sex deviance in the family.

Although dependency conflict factors and role confusing factors were highly correlated, alcoholism rates were higher, holding constant dependency conflict, in the presence of role confusion:

ROLE CONFUSION, DEPENDENCY CONFLICT,[a] AND ALCOHOLISM
(*Per Cent Who Became Alcoholics*)

Role Confusion	Dependency Factors			
	Absent		Present	
Absent	(N: 78)	4	(N: 37)	5
Present	(N: 25)	24	(N: 47)	38

[a] Maternal alternation, escapism, deviance, role resentment; parental antagonism, or denigration of the mother by her husband.

Inadequate role perception in childhood, we believe, would result in a confused self-image, one that would tend to break down in the face of the role requirements imposed upon the average male adult in America.

6

THE INTERACTION OF CAUSES

The evidence produced by this study indicates that a number of causes are at work in the genesis of alcoholism. Parental conflict, control over the uses of alcohol, dependency conflict, and inadequate specification of roles, all appear to have an effect on rates of alcoholism. Because of the size of the sample, it is not possible, of course, to control all the possible variables that may have an influence on alcoholism. Nevertheless, we can gauge the relation of the causal factors that seem to have the greatest importance.

On the one hand, these influences may be divided according to their sources: physiological, cultural, familial. On the other hand, in relation to their probable influence on the child, they may be viewed as producing general stress, dependency conflict, or role confusion. Although we have tended to treat the father's behavior and attitudes as being primarily significant to role confusion and the mother's as being significant to dependency conflict, we are well aware that each of the familial variables related to alcoholism is probably productive of both dependency conflict and role confusion. Thus, the divisions made between them in previous chapters were somewhat arbitrary. In this chapter, we shall investigate some of the interrelationships among the causes of alcoholism that have been considered separately in the preceding chapters.

We shall begin by looking at the interaction of parental religion, social class, and ethnic group. Then we shall turn to the interacting influence of both parents on the child. Finally, we shall examine the cumulative impact of various combinations of these factors.

GENERAL CULTURAL VARIABLES

The separate relation of alcoholism to social class, to religion, and to ethnic background has previously been outlined. Although the number of alcoholics in our sample is small, the effects of these three variables as they interrelate in the backgrounds of alcoholics suggest areas for further study.

In discussing the relatively high alcoholism rates found in America, we have pointed to the importance of middle-class values, which emphasize an ill-defined goal of success to be achieved through masculine independence. In the context of our theory of alcoholism, these values produce both role confusion and dependency conflict.

The pervasive influence of the mass media (and the American school system) in dispersing these values is a factor that cannot be ignored. Some observers consider that the emphasis on success and independence, previously characteristic only of the middle class, has become a general American ethic, shared more or less by all classes. If their view is correct, one would expect few differences in alcoholism rates among native Americans, regardless of their position in the class structure. As the table shows, families of European cultural backgrounds exhibited greater social class differences in rates of alcoholism than did "Yankees."

SOCIAL CLASS, ETHNIC BACKGROUND, AND ALCOHOLISM
(*Per Cent Who Became Alcoholics*)

Social Class[a]	Ethnic Group[b]			
	Yankees		Europeans	
Middle class	(N: 21)	24	(N: 11)	27
Upper-lower class	(N: 21)	19	(N: 41)	15
Lower class	(N: 14)	29	(N: 42)	2

[a] In categorizing the social class of the subjects, the following definitions were used: "middle class," father held professional or white-collar position or had graduated from high school; "upper-lower class," father was a skilled tradesman or had graduated from grammar school; "lower class," father was an unskilled worker and had not completed grammar school.

[b] Families who had lived in the United States for at least three generations were classified as Yankees. Families who had immigrated to the United States within two generations were considered European.

Apparently, native American families tend to accept similar definitions of the masculine role, regardless of social class. In contrast, European immigrants to America—with less opportunity to assimilate the middle-class values of America—show strong social class differences.

The European lower classes, as compared to the Yankees and the European middle class, had significantly lower rates of alcoholism ($P < .01$).[1]

Differently perceived, these American middle-class values might be considered as part of the "Protestant Ethic." One can argue that Catholicism tends to emphasize institutionalism, feminine symbols, resignation, and dependence more than Protestantism. Traditionally, the Protestant emphasis has been on independence and self-reliance. Again, one would expect that Yankees, with their greater exposure to American middle-class values, would tend to accept these Protestant values despite their specific religious convictions. Thus, one would predict that European Catholics would be relatively immune to alcoholism. This expectation proved to be accurate.

RELIGION, ETHNIC BACKGROUND, AND ALCOHOLISM
(*Per Cent Who Became Alcoholics*)

	Yankees		Europeans	
Catholic[a]	(N: 31)	23	(N: 76)	9
Protestant	(N: 25)	24	(N: 18)	17

[a] Subjects were considered Catholic if they professed the Catholic faith.

The European Catholics had a significantly lower rate of alcoholism than did the Yankees or the European Protestants ($P < .05$).[2]

Combining religious, ethnic, and class factors, we found a tendency for the middle class and Yankees from all social classes to be more alcoholic than lower-class Europeans. In addition, we found that Catholic lower-class Europeans had the lowest alcoholism rates ($P < .05$).[3]

RELIGION, SOCIAL CLASS, ETHNIC BACKGROUND, AND ALCOHOLISM
(*Per Cent Who Became Alcoholics*)

	Yankees		Europeans	
	Catholic	Protestant	Catholic	Protestant
Middle class ...	(N: 9) 22	(N: 12) 25	(N: 7) 28	(N: 4) 25
Lower classes ..	(N: 22) 23	(N: 13) 23	(N: 69) 7	(N: 14) 14

Although the numbers are too small to be more than suggestive, it would seem that American values, symbolized in the Protestant middle-class ethic, emphasize "success" and "masculine independence," and thus contribute indirectly to role confusion and dependency conflict. A person whose early experiences made him unsure of his dependent tendencies and was in addition reared to accept these values finds himself in deep conflict.*

PARENTAL ATTITUDES

Although anyone viewing the differential alcoholism rates between America and other countries must acknowledge that some cultural influence contributes to the high rates among Americans, he would still be inclined to ask: *How* do these differences contribute to alcoholism?

In our opinion, American values contribute to alcoholism by increasing role confusion and contributing to dependency conflict among those whose dependency needs have been heightened by their familial environments. Thus, in our view, interpersonal relations within the family are the key to alcoholism.

We have discussed many individual variables within the family that tend to produce alcoholism. In this section, we shall indicate the results of various combinations of these conditions.

We believe that a primary characteristic of alcoholics is that they suffer from heightened dependency needs. Maternal alternation between affection and rejection is especially conducive to the establishment of this trait. Maternal affection as well as rejection, in combination with certain other home conditions, might also be expected to have a similar result. Thus, it is important to examine the interaction between the mother's attitudes and other familial conditions.

Naturally, there was often a striking resemblance between the attitudes of both parents toward their sons. In order to determine if paternal rejection and maternal alternation *independently* influenced alcoholism (or if they were simply reflections of the

---

* Two indirect results emerge from these data. First, one can argue that the material indicates that American social classes do not differ in their definitions of independence and masculinity. Second, it might appear that Catholicism in America has become relatively "Protestantized" and that American Catholics agree with American Protestants in certain basic values.

same pattern), we analyzed the combined effect of these two variables.

PARENTAL ATTITUDES TOWARD BOY AND ALCOHOLISM

(*Per Cent Who Became Alcoholics*)

	Father's Attitude				
Mother's Attitude	Actively Affectionate	Passively Affectionate	Alternating	Passively Rejecting	Actively Rejecting
Actively affectionate	(N: 41) 7	(N: 18) 6	(N: 6) 0	(N: 7) 0	(N: 9) 33
Passively affectionate	(N: 7) 14	(N: 18) 17	(N: 1) 0	(N: 4) 25	(N: 3) 33
Alternating	(N: 4) 25	(N: 6) 50	(N: 2) 50	(N: 2) 0	(N: 3) 33
Passively rejecting	(N: 1) 0	(N: 2) 0	(N: 3) 0	(N: 5) 40	(N: 3) 0
Actively rejecting	(N: 1) 0	(N: 1) 0	(N: 2) 50	(N: 1) 0	(N: 2) 50

As can be seen, there was a strong correlation between maternal and paternal attitudes toward the child. Therefore, the numbers in many categories are extremely small.

To make possible statistical treatment of the material, we grouped these specific combinations of parental attitudes into three "types" of families. These "types" were divided according to the presumed impact they would have in producing dependency conflict:

1. Families that satisfied the child's dependency needs. These were families in which the mother demonstrated active affection toward the child and the father was, at the minimum, not actively rejecting.

2. Families that frustrated dependency needs, without necessarily creating a dependency conflict in the child. This category was composed of boys with rejecting mothers, and those whose mothers were passively affectionate and whose fathers were not actively rejecting.

3. Families that heightened the boy's dependency conflict by frustrating and also appeasing his dependency needs. In these

families the mother was ambivalent; or the father was actively rejecting and the mother was affectionate.

Using the three divisions, we found the highest alcoholism rates among families that produced heightened dependency conflict and the lowest rates of alcoholism among families that tended to satisfy dependency needs ($P < .01$).[4]

DEPENDENCY AND ALCOHOLISM

	Per Cent Who Became Alcoholics
Satisfied dependency needs (N: 72)	6
Frustrated dependency needs (N: 51)	18
Conflict over dependency (N: 29)	34

A father's absence from the home often results in the child's greater dependence on the mother. The effects of paternal absence, one might expect, depend largely on the mother's attitudes. To see the relation of these factors to alcoholism, we examined the combined impact of paternal absence and maternal attitudes:

PATERNAL ABSENCE, MOTHER'S ATTITUDE TOWARD BOY, AND ALCOHOLISM
(Per Cent Who Became Alcoholics)

Mother's Attitude	Father Present		Father Absent	
Actively affectionate	(N: 61)	5	(N: 30)	13
Passively affectionate	(N: 27)	15	(N: 9)	33
Rejecting	(N: 15)	20	(N: 6)	33
Alternating	(N: 15)	33	(N: 6)	33

This table points again to the importance of dependency conflict in the backgrounds of alcoholics. One third of the sons of overtly ambivalent women, whether the father was present or absent, became alcoholics. There was also a tendency for paternal absence to result in higher alcoholism rates despite maternal affection. Among those whose fathers were absent, the alcoholism rates for sons of actively affectionate women did not differ significantly from the rates for sons of women who were not actively affectionate. Among those whose fathers were present, however, we found that men who had actively affectionate mothers had significantly lower rates of alcoholism ($P < .01$).[5] Thus, the mother's attitude had a greater impact on alcoholism rates when the father was present in the home than when he was absent. Paternal absence heightens the boy's dependence on the mother (as does maternal ambivalence). We believe that conflict arises when the masculine role must be assumed in later adult life. To further substantiate this hypothesis, we divided the families somewhat differently:

1. Families in which dependency needs were satisfied (father present and mother actively affectionate).

2. Families in which the boy's dependence on the mother was heightened, but dependency needs were not frustrated (father absent, mother actively affectionate).

3. Families in which dependency needs were frustrated, but dependence on mother was not heightened (father present, mother passive or rejecting).

4. Families in which dependency on the mother was heightened and dependency needs were frustrated (father absent and mother not actively affectionate or mother overtly ambivalent in her attitude toward the boy).

The relationship of this dependency-frustration scale to alcoholism can be seen in the following table:

DEPENDENCY FRUSTRATION AND ALCOHOLISM

	Per Cent Who Became Alcoholics
Dependency needs satisfied (N: 61)	5
Maternal dependence heightened (N.: 30)	13
Dependency needs frustrated (N: 42)	17
Maternal dependence heightened and frustrated (N: 36)	33

Alcoholism rates increased progressively from a low, if dependency needs were satisfied, to a high, if they were both heightened and frustrated ($P < .001$).[6]

In the preceding analysis, we have noted that paternal absence tends to heighten dependence on the mother, which may under some conditions result in dependency conflict. If the father is present in the home, dependency conflict can arise from other sources; one would expect, for example, that mothers who reject their sons and who have low esteem for their husbands would be likely to create conflict in the son. One would assume that attacks on the father's worth would heighten the boy's dependence on the mother. In such a situation (if the mother failed to satisfy the boy's dependency needs), conflict over dependency might well result. The following table shows the interaction between the mother's esteem for her husband and her attitude toward her son as they relate to alcoholism rates:

MOTHER'S ESTEEM FOR FATHER, HER ATTITUDE TOWARD
BOY, AND ALCOHOLISM

(*Per Cent Who Became Alcoholics*)

Mother's Attitude toward Boy	Mother's Esteem for Father			
	Moderate or High		Low	
Actively affectionate	(N: 52)	8	(N: 35)	9
Passively affectionate	(N: 19)	16	(N: 12)	33
Alternating	(N: 11)	18	(N: 11)	55
Rejecting	(N: 13)	15	(N: 9)	22

Except for the sons of actively affectionate women, the boys whose mothers had little esteem for their husbands had higher alcoholism rates than those whose mothers had moderate or high esteem for their husbands. Again, the numbers are too small for individual statistical comparisons. If one compares the three major types of families—those in which the mother actively loved her son, as opposed to those in which the mother was unaffectionate but admired the father and to those in which the mother rejected both her son and her husband—a highly significant difference emerges ($P < .001$).[7]

By looking at the father's attitude to his son, at paternal absence, and at the mother's esteem for the father—in relation to the mother's attitude to the child—we found two types of backgrounds particularly productive of alcoholism: (*a*) The combination of maternal affection with rejection by either the mother or the father was strongly related to alcoholism; and (*b*) Maternal passivity or rejection coupled with paternal absence or low maternal esteem for the husband resulted in high rates of alcoholism.

THE CUMULATIVE IMPACT

In the first section of this chapter we analyzed the relationship of cultural variables to alcoholism and in the second, of parental variables to alcoholism. In this section, we shall examine how stress, dependency conflict, and role confusion, as well as such "channeling" factors as social class and religion, affect alcoholism rates.

We have argued that neurological disorder, familial conflict, and sexual deviance within the family produce general stress in the child. We have argued that these conditions do not lead directly to alcoholism, but that they must be mediated by other influences that direct deviance into the specific alcoholic pattern. Although we have discussed dependency conflict and role confusion as separable causes of alcoholism, we have pointed out that these are interrelated conditions which are directly relevant to the production of an "alcoholism-prone personality."

The interrelationship of stress, dependency conflict, role confusion, and alcoholism is shown in the following chart: *

STRESS, DEPENDENCY CONFLICT, ROLE CONFUSION, AND ALCOHOLISM
(Per Cent Who Became Alcoholics)

	Stress		No Stress	
Dependency conflict and				
role confusion	(N: 35)	43	(N: 12)	25
Role confusion	(N: 5)	0	(N: 20)	30
Dependency conflict	(N: 19)	5	(N: 18)	6
Neither	(N: 12)	0	(N: 66)	5

This analysis of the interrelationship of stress, dependency conflict, role confusion, and alcoholism leads to two conclusions: (1) that "stress backgrounds" were not directly related to alcoholism rates, and (2) that "stress backgrounds" were strongly related to dependency conflict variables. Seventy-three per cent of those with role confusion and dependency conflict, 51 per cent with de-

* "Stress" indicates at least one of the following in the boy's background: parental conflict, sex deviance in family, neural disorder. "Dependency conflict" indicates at least one of the following: maternal ambivalence, maternal role ambiguity, maternal deviance, maternal escapism, parental antagonism, paternal denigration of mother. "Role confusion" indicates paternal antagonism or escapism or a conflicting outsider with an absence of high demands.

pendency conflict only, and only 17 per cent of those without dependency conflict had stress backgrounds (P < .001).[8] Therefore, stress appears to be related to alcoholism primarily because parental conflict, sexual deviance in the family, or neural disorder of the child seem to lead the parents to behave in such a way as to promote dependency conflict.

In discussing cultural variables, we pointed to the Protestant ethic, or middle-class values, as leading to alcoholism. In contrast, it would appear that the greater Catholic emphasis on subordination and resignation tends to militate against alcoholism. To test the importance of these variables in relation to dependency conflict and role confusion, we examined their interacting effects.

SOCIAL CLASS, RELIGION,
DEPENDENCY CONFLICT, ROLE CONFUSION, AND ALCOHOLISM

(*Per Cent Who Became Alcoholics*)

	Non-Catholic		Catholic[a]	
	Middle Class	Lower Class	Middle Class	Lower Class
Role confusion and dependency conflict	(N: 9) 44	(N: 31) 39	————	(N: 7) 28
Role confusion or dependency conflict	(N: 14) 21	(N: 35) 14	(N: 1) 0	(N: 12) 0
Neither	(N: 8) 13	(N: 44) 5	(N: 4) 0	(N: 22) 0

[a] Subjects were considered Catholic only if their mothers attended Mass at least once a week.

These relationships again indicate that religion and middle-class values channel dependency-role conflict in a way uniquely pertinent to the production of alcoholic-prone personalities. Dependency conflict and role confusion, when found in combination, resulted in the highest alcoholism rates when religion and social class were held constant. On the other hand, when dependency conflict and role confusion were held constant, Catholics had the lowest and the non-Catholic middle class had the highest alcoholism rates.

As has been indicated in previous chapters, alcoholism rates were highest among subjects whose backgrounds contained the greatest number of factors related to alcoholism. To assess the

cumulative impact on adult alcoholism of the seventeen variables*
discussed under the categories of stress, channeling factors, dependency conflict, and role confusion, we counted the number of
these factors found in the childhood background of each subject.
*As the number of these "negative" factors increased, alcoholism
rates progressively increased.*

THE CUMULATIVE IMPACT OF SEVENTEEN FACTORS RELATED TO ALCOHOLISM

Number of Factors	Per Cent Who Became Alcoholics
0 (N: 5)	0
1–2 (N: 59)	3
3–4 (N: 55)	11
5–6 (N: 31)	13
7–8 (N: 22)	23
9–10 (N: 12)	75
11–13 (N: 3)	100

Perhaps the most striking finding, despite the very small numbers, is the fact that every alcoholic had at least one of these factors in his background and that each of the three cases with more
than ten of these factors did become alcoholic.

The relationship between childhood variables and later alcoholism suggests that an accurate prediction of alcoholism may
be possible years before the symptoms appear. Thus we attempted
to select "critical" variables that most strikingly differentiated the
alcoholics from the nondeviants. A scoring system was devised
that gave equal weight to five factors: maternal alternation, maternal deviance, paternal antagonism, parental escapism, and an
"outsider" in conflict with parental values. Because of its positive
impact, one point was subtracted from the child's negative score
if he was raised in a family that subjected him to high demands.
These were the six factors that seemed most likely to indicate those
who had become alcoholics.

* Middle class, non-Catholicism, parental conflict, neural disorder, sex
deviance, maternal ambivalence, maternal deviance, maternal escapism,
father's low esteem for mother, parental antagonism, maternal resentment of
role, paternal antagonism toward boy, paternal escapism, low demands, subnormal maternal restrictiveness, absence of supervision. No child was subject
to more than 13 negative factors.

SIX CRITICAL VARIABLES AND ALCOHOLISM

Score		Per Cent Who Became Alcoholics
Zero	(N: 97)	4
One	(N: 44)	16
Two	(N: 33)	21
Three	(N: 11)	82
Four	(N: 2)	100

A zero score was reflected in an extremely low rate of alcoholism; a score of three or four was reflected in an extremely high rate of alcoholism; between these extremes, approximately one out of six subjects had become an alcoholic (P < .001).[9]

As a final assessment of the effects of childhood background on alcoholism, we were able to identify four types of families that, within the scope of the sample, produced *only* alcoholic sons. Two of these types were composed of mothers who probably developed dependency conflicts in the child and fathers who probably promoted role confusion. Specifically, these families were those in which (a) the mothers were overtly ambivalent and deviant and not strongly Catholic, the fathers were antagonistic or escapist or denigrated their wives, and low demands were imposed upon the son; or (b) the mothers were escapist and not strongly Catholic, and the fathers were antagonistic toward their sons. Of the nine subjects who had one of these backgrounds, all became alcoholics.

A second group of families could be roughly described as strongly promoting dependency conflict and role confusion through the influence of an outsider. Specifically, these families were of two types: (1) those in which an outsider was in conflict with parental values and which also contained an antagonistic-escapist father, or (2) those in which an outsider was in conflict with parental values and also contained an overtly ambivalent or deviant or escapist mother. All six subjects who had these backgrounds became alcoholics.

If a prediction had been made that all, and only, those boys raised in one of these four types of family environments would become alcoholics prior to middle age, this prediction would have been 93 per cent accurate.[10]

Although the relationship is by no means perfect—inadequate information, unreliable raters' judgments, and other defects prevented total accuracy—the pattern suggests that these early conditions were strongly associated with the onset of adult alcoholism.

The various analyses presented in this section lead to the conclusion that alcoholic behavior is, to a high degree, the result of factors that can be ascertained in childhood. We have argued that these influences, particularly in a culture that sets a premium on masculine independence, contribute to alcoholism by heightening dependency conflict and by creating a confused self-image.

7

ALCOHOLISM AND CRIMINALITY

In the previous chapters, we have offered the opinion that dependency conflict and role confusion are dominant in the causal backgrounds of alcoholics. Yet the reader may well ask: Are they really related to *alcoholism*, or are these same pathological conditions found generally in the backgrounds of most social deviants?

This chapter is aimed toward giving at least a partial answer to this question by comparing the backgrounds of two forms of deviants—alcoholics and criminals—as they differ from men who are neither alcoholics nor criminals.

Before beginning this comparison, let us specify the criteria we used in diagnosing a man as an alcoholic, as a criminal, or as an alcoholic criminal.

Anyone who committed a "major" antisocial act—that is, an act which might, if detected, be punishable by incarceration—we considered as criminal. Operationally, we classified as criminal any of our subjects who had been convicted by the courts in Massachusetts for assault, theft (larceny, automobile theft, or breaking and entering), or sex crimes.

We believe that a standard based on court convictions is probably the most objective measure of criminality because the possibility of personal biases is most limited. Arrests may be subject to the prejudices of police officers and incarceration is frequently subject to the judge's appraisal of home conditions and other biasing factors. Self-report techniques leave open the possibility of two contradictory forms of misinformation: boastfulness (reporting of crimes not committed) or deception (failure to report crimes actually committed).

In this book, we have defined an alcoholic as "one whose drinking has become the source of community or family difficulties or one who has recognized that excessive drinking is a primary problem to him." Operationally, we classified as alcoholics those of our subjects who had been members of Alcoholics Anonymous, those who had been committed to a hospital for alcoholism, those who had sought aid from a public welfare agency because of drinking, and those who had been convicted by the courts at least twice for drunkenness.

In previous chapters, we have been concerned with differentiating the alcoholics from the nondeviants—that is, from the 158 men who were neither alcoholics nor criminals. Partly because we focused upon alcoholism as a generic disorder, but more importantly because the backgrounds of the alcoholic criminals were so similar to those of the noncriminal alcoholics, we considered the criminal alcoholics as primarly alcoholic and as secondarily criminal. In this chapter, we will mention the few characteristics that distinguish the criminal and the noncriminal alcoholics.

We classified the eleven alcoholics who had not been convicted for any major crime as *noncriminal alcoholics*. We considered as *criminal alcoholics* the eighteen alcoholics who had been convicted for major crimes: one for assault, eleven for theft, one for sex crimes, and five for some combination of these.[1]

We classified forty-four men as *nonalcoholic criminals* (referred to simply as "criminals"). These men showed no evidence of alcoholism; they had been convicted by the courts at least once for a major nondrinking offense and had not been convicted for drunkenness: two had been convicted for assault, thirty-four for theft, six for sex crimes, and two for some combination of these crimes.

We omitted from the analyses the twenty-four subjects who had been convicted once for drunkenness. We believe they could not be classified as either alcoholic or nonalcoholic with any degree of confidence.

The problem of differentiating various forms of deviance has long concerned the social scientists. Assuming that alcoholism and criminality have been adequately distinguished, what are the similarities and the dissimilarities in their origins? What leads one person to become an alcoholic and another to become a criminal?

We will not attempt an extensive analysis of the causes of criminality; that was the subject of a previous report on the project.[2] Rather, we hope to differentiate between *nonalcoholic* criminals and alcoholics. We will attempt to describe the factors that either generally predispose a person toward deviance or tend to channel his deviance.

If we hypothesize that social deviance serves a psychological function for a person, we can expect to find fundamental differences between the early backgrounds of deviants and nondeviants. Furthermore, we could expect to find differences among various types of deviants. In fact, we have noted that certain variables correlate both with alcoholism and with nonalcoholic criminality; yet the specific backgrounds for these two types of deviants present quite different syndromes. Through analyzing these differences, we hope to clarify the nature of alcoholism as a *specific* form of social deviance.

This chapter will be divided into several sections. In the first of these, we will discuss the conditions that do *not* differentiate the alcoholics from the criminals but do differentiate both criminals and alcoholics from nondeviants. In the other sections, we will turn to the "channeling conditions" that tend to lead a person toward alcoholism rather than criminality or toward criminality rather than alcoholism. In other words, we will be showing that some factors are generally found in the backgrounds of at least two types of deviants, but that other factors—considered as particularly productive of alcoholism—are *not* generally found in the backgrounds of criminals. We believe that in this chapter the relevancy of dependency conflict and inadequate role specification to the genesis of alcoholism will again be demonstrated.

PREDISPOSING FACTORS OF DEVIANCE

One of the most important questions in studying the causes of deviance concerns the "choice of symptoms." It is frequently argued that only knowledge of the adult situation or of personal preferences can lead to predicting accurately the form the deviance will take. Many of the conditions that have been shown to relate to adult alcoholism, we realize, are also related to adult criminality; yet other conditions are significantly related only to alcoholism or only to criminality. We hypothesized that the predisposing factors operate by producing tension and stress which, when combined with certain unsatisfied needs, lead to alcoholism, and when combined with different frustrations lead to criminality. In this section, we will discuss the conditions that clearly distinguish the nondeviants from the deviants, but that do not differentiate the alcoholics from the criminals.

In Chapter 3, we discussed certain predisposing conditions of alcoholism. Two of these factors, parental conflict and neural disorder, also figured prominently in the backgrounds of criminals. In disproportionate numbers, the criminals were exposed to intense parental conflict (P < .005)[3] and showed definite signs of neural disorder (P < .05).[4] Thus, neither parental conflict nor neural disorder can be said to have a specific causal relationship to alcoholism.

Three additional stress-producing conditions tended to underlie social deviance in general, yet did not differentiate between the backgrounds of alcoholics and those of criminals.

1. Criminals, as well as alcoholics, differed significantly from the nondeviant subjects in that they more often came from families in which sexual deviance had occurred (P < .005).[5] There were thirty-eight families included in the study who could be considered sexually deviant (in the sense that either an illegitimate child was a member of the family or that one of the children was a victim of incest); 57 per cent of the subjects who had been raised in such environments had become either alcoholics or criminals.

2. Criminals had been subjected significantly more often than nondeviants to the submerged resentment accompanying role ambiguity on the part of the mother (P < .005).[6] Of the thirty-six boys whose mothers were ambiguous in their familial role 72 per cent had become either alcoholics or criminals.

3. In defining criminal behavior (as measured by court convictions), alcoholism, or sexual promiscuity as "deviant," we found that maternal deviance was significantly related to alcoholism. Maternal deviance was also strongly related to criminality (P < .001).[7] Sixty-six per cent of the twenty-nine subjects who had deviant mothers became either alcoholics or criminals.

The importance of the conditions underlying deviance can be seen in a comparison of the proportions of deviants (both alcoholic and criminal) to nondeviants who had each of these factors in their backgrounds.

PREDISPOSING FACTORS IN THE CAUSATION OF DEVIANCE[a]
(*Subjects about whom there was no information were omitted*)

Background	Per Cent of Alcoholic Deviants	Per Cent of Criminal Deviants	Per Cent of Nondeviants
Parental conflict	(N: 23) 52	(N: 38) 52	(N: 134) 27
Neural disorder	(N: 29) 17	(N: 44) 18	(N: 158) 6
Sex deviance in family ..	(N: 29) 31	(N: 44) 30	(N: 158) 10
Maternal role ambiguity.	(N: 29) 28	(N: 42) 43	(N: 152) 7
Maternal deviance	(N: 29) 31	(N: 42) 33	(N: 155) 12

[a] A higher proportion of the alcoholics and of the criminals than of the nondeviants had each of these factors in their backgrounds.

The chart indicates that each of these predisposing factors was found from two to five times as frequently in the backgrounds of deviants as of nondeviants.

The effects of these tension-producing conditions—neurological disorder, parental conflict, incest or illegitimacy in the family, "martyrdom" of the mother, and maternal deviance—appear to be cumulative. For if one computes the deviance percentages of the subjects who had between zero and five of these factors in their backgrounds, the rate of deviance (either alcoholic or criminal) steadily increases.

STRESS AND DEVIANCE

Number of Predisposing Factors	Per Cent Who Became Deviants
0 (N: 116)	20
1 (N: 47)	23
2 (N: 36)	44
3 (N: 23)	61
4 (N: 7)	100
5 (N: 2)	100

Thus, it appears that the greater the stress, the more likely it is that deviance will occur.

Whereas neural disorder, parental conflict, maternal "martyrdom," and deviance had positive relationships to both alcoholism and criminality, maternal warmth was negatively related to both forms of deviance. Of the 111 boys raised by warm mothers, only 7 per cent became alcoholics (P < .005)[8] and 11 per cent became criminals (P < .001).[9]

It might reasonably be assumed that a child who receives warm attention and love from his mother would tend to feel less tension than would a child whose mother was not actively affectionate.

When maternal warmth and the predisposing factors of deviance are both taken into account, this pattern emerges:

MATERNAL WARMTH, STRESS, AND DEVIANCE

Number of Pre-disposing Factors	Warm Mother Per Cent Who Be-came Deviants		Mother Not Warm Per Cent Who Be-came Deviants	
0–1	(N: 92)	13	(N: 67)	30
2–3	(N: 18)	39	(N: 42)	57
4–5	(N: 1)	100	(N: 8)	100

Deviance rates ranged from a low of 13 per cent among the ninety-one men who had been raised by warm mothers in families that were unlikely to produce general stress, to a high of 100 per cent among the nine men who had backgrounds most likely to produce general stress.

Both the absence of maternal warmth and the number of stress-producing factors were significantly related to deviance. Among those raised by warm mothers, deviance rates were significantly higher if there had been more than one stress-producing condition (P < .01).[10] Similarly, among those whose mothers were not warm, the presence of more than one stress-producing factor resulted in significantly higher rates of deviance (P < .001).[11]

Looking at the effects of maternal warmth with stress-producing factors held constant, we found that among those who had zero or only one predisposing condition a significantly lower proportion who had been raised by warm mothers had become deviants (P < .01).[12] Maternal warmth seems also to have reduced pressure toward deviance among those with two or more predisposing factors (non-significant). In the presence of general stress, maternal warmth seems to be less effective as a preventive to deviance.

Although none of these stress-producing conditions differentiated the alcoholics from the criminals, the fact that they did differentiate each group from the nondeviant population suggests that they produced the tensions leading to social deviance.

A variety of reasons could be offered for this phenomenon. It might be most reasonably argued that all of these influences—parental conflict, neural disorder, sex deviance in the family, maternal role resentment, and maternal deviance—created a high level of inner stress and tension which led to a general inability to tolerate the usual frustrations of adult life. The expression of this stress in a particular form of deviance was, however, guided by other factors.

In the following sections, we will discuss the channeling influences that distinguished between alcoholics and nonalcoholic criminals as well as those that differentiated the noncriminal alcoholics from the criminal alcoholics.

CHANNELING FACTORS: TYPE OF EMOTIONAL FRUSTRATION

Almost everyone familiar with research on the causes of crime acknowledges the importance of emotional frustration as one early source of criminality. In Chapter 4 we stressed the importance of dependency conflict—as instigated by emotional frustration—to the genesis of alcoholism. In this section, we hope to show that the specific nature of the early emotional frustration plays a prominent role in determining the type of social deviance.

The evidence indicates that emotional frustrations that produce conflict—a desire to be loved coupled with a fear concerning the satisfaction of this desire—is particularly related to alcoholism. Criminals, on the other hand, are typically victimized by cold, emotionally barren environments—a situation tending to extinguish dependency desires through continuing and complete frustration.

The Mother's Attitude Toward Her Son

Heightened dependency conflict would most likely occur when a boy's mother alternates between overt affection and overt rejection. This form of ambivalent behavior tends to inflate the mother's importance as a source of gratification while, at the same time, it fails to satisfy the aroused need. Maternal rejection, also emotionally frustrating, would be expected to have a greater tendency to extinguish desires for dependency. The relationship between the mother's attitude toward her son and rates of deviance can be seen in the tabulation below:

MOTHER'S ATTITUDE TOWARD BOY AND TYPE OF DEVIANCE

Mother's Attitude	Per Cent Who Became Alcoholics	Per Cent Who Became Criminals
Actively affectionate (N: 111)	7	11
Passively affectionate (N: 51)	14	27
Rejecting (N: 36)	14	33
Alternating (N: 28)	29	18

As can be seen, maternal alternation was significantly related to high alcoholism rates ($P < .02$), although it was *not* significantly related to criminality. On the other hand, maternal rejection was significantly related to criminality ($P < .02$),[13] but was not to alcoholism.*

Alcoholics and criminals have typically suffered emotional frustration; the nature of this frustration—and, presumably, the resultant personality—was different. This contrast between alcoholics and criminals in terms of their emotional backgrounds appears again in the comparative analysis of the effects of the mother's attitude toward her son in united and in broken homes:

MATERNAL AFFECTION, PATERNAL ABSENCE, AND
TYPE OF DEVIANCE

	Per Cent Who Became Alcoholics	Per Cent Who Became Criminals
Father present		
Mother affectionate (N: 102)	7	14
Mother not affectionate (N: 36)	22	17
Father absent		
Mother affectionate (N: 48)	15	19
Mother not affectionate (N: 23)	17	48

* The five alcoholics with rejecting mothers were criminal alcoholics.

It is interesting to note that both the lowest and the highest alcoholism rates occurred in united homes ($P < .02$).[14] Alcoholism rates varied only slightly in response to maternal attitudes if the father was absent.

Conversely, criminal rates varied only slightly in united homes, but strongly reflected the maternal attitude when the father had been absent (P < .01).[15]

On the basis of these facts, we feel justified in arguing that conflict over dependency desires is basic to alcoholism and that a subnormal dependency drive is more fundamental to the genesis of criminality. This hypothesis is based on a theory that some dependency drive is aroused in early infancy through the essential maternal care requisite in maintaining life. Three things, we propose, can happen to this drive: (1) it can be satisfied, and therefore remain at a relatively constant level; (2) it can be erratically satisfied or tantalized, therefore either increasing and producing conflict during adulthood (due to requirements imposed by society) or arousing a desire for its suppression due to fear of frustration; or (3) it can be consistently frustrated, and therefore tend to be extinguished.

In a united family, especially if the father too was affectionate, maternal affection should generally produce satisfaction of dependency desires. Among such families, both alcoholism and criminality were relatively infrequent.

In a united family in which the mother was not affectionate, the father would be a *potential* source of affection. This possibility of gaining dependency-drive satisfaction tends to maintain dependency drive while giving rise to conflict over dependency. Alcoholism rates were higher than criminal rates only among such families.*

A child raised by a rejecting mother who was the sole potential source of affection would be most likely to undergo dependency-drive extinction. In families marked by the absence of the father, criminal rates were extremely high if the mother had not been affectionate.†

* Although the numbers are small, we found that among united families alcoholism rates varied from 4 per cent for those with actively affectionate mothers to 29 per cent for those with alternating mothers. The criminality rates were 9 per cent and 12 per cent, respectively.

† In fact, among the fourteen boys whose mothers were consistently rejecting and whose fathers were absent, eight had become nonalcoholic criminals and two had become alcoholic criminals.

We have emphasized that the mother's attitude toward her child seems to be important in producing deviant behavior. In Chapter 6, we utilized a scale based upon the attitudes of both parents toward their son as these attitudes would theoretically be related to dependency drive. We proposed that the child's dependency needs would probably be satisfied if the mother was actively affectionate and if the father was not actively rejecting. We proposed that a child whose mother was rejecting or only passively affectionate (so long as the father was not actively rejecting) would probably have his dependency drive extinguished through consistent frustration. And we suggested that a child whose mother was ambivalent (regardless of his father's attitude) or whose mother was affectionate and father overtly rejecting would probably develop conflict over dependency desires. The alcoholic and criminal rates for these three types of families show an interesting difference:

DEPENDENCY AND TYPE OF DEVIANCE

	Per Cent Who Became Alcoholics	Per Cent Who Became Criminals
Satisfied dependency needs (N: 81)	5	11
Frustrated dependency needs (N: 74) ..	12	31
Conflict over dependency (N: 36)	28	19

Alcoholism rates were lowest among families who tended to satisfy dependency needs and highest among those who tended to create conflict over dependency (P < .01). Criminal rates were also lowest among families who tended to satisfy dependency needs, but were highest among families whose attitudes would be most likely to extinguish dependency desires (P < .005).[16]

To put these findings somewhat differently, boys whose dependency needs were rather consistently frustrated were more likely to become criminals than alcoholics; boys in whom there was both satisfaction and frustration of dependency desires were more apt to become alcoholics than criminals (P < .05).[17]

The Mother's Reaction to Crises

In Chapter 4, we pointed out that mothers who, when faced with crises, changed the subject, withdrew to their rooms, became promiscuous, or in other ways reacted by escapism produced alcoholic sons more often than did women who were either unrealistically aggressive or realistic in their reactions to crises (P < .02). We suggested that this escapist behavior of the mothers would be likely to increase dependency conflict because the child would be uncertain about receiving his mother's support when it might be needed. This particular form—escapism—of reaction to crises was not significantly related to criminality. Nevertheless, a mother who reacted unrealistically to crises through aggression, desertion, or escapism was more likely to have a criminal son than one who reacted realistically (P < .005):[18]

MOTHER'S REACTION TO CRISES AND TYPE OF DEVIANCE

Mother's Reaction to Crises	Per Cent Who Became Alcoholics	Per Cent Who Became Criminals
Realistic (N: 125)	13	16
Aggressive (N: 30)	10	27
Desertion (N: 6)	0	67
Escapist (N: 32)	28	25

Although only six mothers actually deserted their families, it is perhaps worth noting that five of their sons became criminals and none became alcoholics. On the other hand, escapist behavior was more likely to lead to alcoholism. One would be inclined to say that a child whose mother deserts in times of crises would know that he could not count on his mother, whereas one whose mother remained in the home and yet "escaped" would be more uncertain regarding her possible support.

The Mother's Discipline of Her Son

In attempting to control their children, parents use many techniques. These may or may not be "alienating." That is, they may drive the child away from the disciplinarian. We had divided disciplinary techniques into two types: punitive (based on force and power) and nonpunitive (based upon withdrawal of approval or reasoning).

A contrast appeared in alcoholism and criminal rates when we examined the influence of the mother's disciplinary techniques (holding constant the fact that she was the major disciplinarian):

MOTHER'S DISCIPLINE AND TYPE OF DEVIANCE

Mother's Technique of Discipline	Per Cent Who Became Alcoholics	Per Cent Who Became Criminals
Punitive (N: 66)	9	21
Nonpunitive (N: 66)	17	5

The punitive techniques probably antagonized the boy, alienated him from his mother. Under these circumstances, criminality occurred significantly more frequently than among boys whose mothers used nonpunitive techniques of discipline (P < .05).[19] Punitive discipline by the mother did not, however, lead to alcoholism.

We can see from the table that, if the mother used punitive discipline, her son was less likely to become an alcoholic than a criminal; if she used nonpunitive techniques, he was more likely to become an alcoholic than a criminal* (P < .025).[20]

Again, this evidence suggests that the alcoholic's dependency needs are probably greater than the criminal's—for it seems reasonable to assume that if the mother was the primary disciplinarian, her punitiveness would tend to extinguish dependent desires.

The Mother's Relationship to Her Husband

The general emotional tone of a family is largely governed by the nature of the relationship between the parents. We rated the parents as being affectionate, indifferent, or antagonistic toward one another. We have already shown that alcoholism was significantly related to parental antagonism (P < .02). The statistics of the comparative effects of the three types of parental environments on alcoholic and criminal rates are as follows:

RELATIONSHIP BETWEEN PARENTS AND TYPE OF DEVIANCE

Relationship Between Parents	Per Cent Who Became Alcoholics	Per Cent Who Became Criminals
Affectionate (N: 106)	11	12
Indifferent (N: 23)	4	39
Antagonistic (N: 50)	22	26

* Among the forty boys whose mothers used nonpunitive techniques with consistency (i.e., regularly disapproved particular actions), 20 per cent became alcoholics and only 3 per cent became criminals.

Parental antagonism was productive of criminality as well as alcoholism. Yet criminal rates were highest among those whose parents were indifferent (P < .05)[21]—a type of environment that produced little alcoholism. These emotionally barren homes, one might expect, would provide little satisfaction to dependency desires.

Summary: Type of Emotional Frustration and Type of Deviance

We have shown that criminals and alcoholics, although similar in that they have experienced emotional frustrations, have been reared in quite different environments. Specifically, we have shown that:

1. Whereas maternal ambivalence was significantly related to alcoholism, maternal rejection was related to criminality.

2. Whereas absence of maternal affection resulted in alcoholism if the father was present in the home, it was productive of criminality if the father was absent.

3. Whereas the attitudes of the father and the mother toward their son were significantly related to alcoholism when they produced a conflict over dependency desires, they were significantly related to criminality when they extinguished dependency desires.

4. Whereas maternal escapism was significantly related to alcoholism, it was not significantly related to criminality.

5. Whereas boys disciplined nonpunitively by their mothers were more likely to become alcoholics than criminals, those disciplined punitively were more likely to become criminals than alcoholics.

6. Whereas parental antagonism was particularly productive of alcoholism, parental indifference was more productive of criminality.

These comparisons are illustrated in the following table, which shows the proportions of alcoholics, criminals, and nondeviants who had experienced each of these various forms of emotional frustration:

TYPE OF EMOTIONAL FRUSTRATION AND TYPE OF DEVIANCE

(*Subjects about whom there was no information were omitted*)

Background	Per Cent of Alcoholics	Per Cent of Nonalcoholic Criminals	Per Cent of Nondeviants
Maternal ambivalence ..	(N: 28) 29[a]	(N: 43) 12	(N: 155) 10[a]
Maternal rejection	(N: 28) 18	(N: 43) 28[a]	(N: 155) 12[a]
If father present, mother not affectionate	(N: 15) 53[a]	(N: 20) 30	(N: 103) 21[a]
If father absent, mother not affectionate	(N: 11) 36	(N: 20) 55[a]	(N: 40) 20[a]
Parental attitudes productive of dependency conflict	(N: 23) 43[a]	(N: 39) 18	(N: 129) 15[a]
Parental attitudes tending to extinguish dependent desires	(N: 23) 39	(N: 39) 59[a]	(N: 129) 33[a]
Maternal escapism	(N: 28) 32[a]	(N: 40) 20	(N: 125) 12[a]
If mother major disciplinarian, punitive	(N: 17) 35[b]	(N: 19) 74[a,b]	(N: 96) 48[a]
Parental antagonism ...	(N: 24) 46[a]	(N: 35) 37	(N: 120) 22[a]
Parental indifference ...	(N: 24) 4	(N: 35) 26[a]	(N: 120) 11[a]

[a] Significant differences are noted, the superior [a] marking the two groups compared.

[b] This difference also was significant.

The alcoholics* had been subjected to conditions that would be expected to lead to dependency conflict: maternal ambivalence, absence of maternal affection with the father present in the home, paternal rejection coupled with maternal affection, maternal escapism, and parental antagonism. The criminals, on the other hand, had experienced what, perhaps, can best be explained in terms of the extinction of dependency drive: maternal rejection (especially if the father was absent from the home), punitive discipline by the mother, and parental indifference.

CHANNELING FACTORS: ROLE SPECIFICATION

In Chapter 5, under the rubric of "inadequate role specification," we described those findings which indicated that alcoholics had reason either to reject their paternal models or to fail to per-

* The criminal and the noncriminal alcoholics did not differ significantly with respect to any of these variables.

ceive the male role clearly. This background, we found, was not characteristic of the criminals. Rather, criminality seems to be at least partially a response to identification with a deviant role model.*

Inadequate Perception of the Male Role and Alcoholism

We have set forth findings which we believe indicate that the alcoholic's background inadequately prepares him to accept the adult male role and leaves him with a confused self-image. Many of the following conditions, which significantly differentiated the alcoholic from the nondeviant, did not differentiate the criminal from the nondeviant. Each condition, however, would tend to lead to role confusion.

1. A significantly higher proportion of the alcoholics had been raised in families in which an adult who was in conflict with the parents played a guiding role for the child (P < .005). The conflicting demands imposed upon the child would, we assume, result in the child's confusion over expectations. This type of family background did not produce a high proportion of criminals.

2. A significantly higher proportion of the alcoholics had fathers who "escaped" when faced with crises (P < .025). Since the cultural definition of the male role seems to embody the ability to face crises, the son of a father who escaped under these circumstances would be likely, we believe, either to reject his paternal model or to remain confused in his perception of the masculine role. Although paternal "escapism" was not significantly related to criminality, there was a tendency for any "deviant" reaction to crises by the father to be related to crime.

FATHER'S REACTION TO CRISES AND TYPE OF DEVIANCE

	Per Cent Who Became Alcoholics	Per Cent Who Became Criminals
Realistic reaction to crises (N: 60)....	8	15
Aggressive reaction to crises (N: 27)....	7	33
Escapist reaction to crises (N: 76)....	18	26

3. A significantly lower proportion of the alcoholics had been raised in families that imposed high demands (P < .01). High

* For a more complete discussion, see Joan McCord and William McCord, "The Effects of Parental Role Model on Criminality," *The Journal of Social Issues* (Vol. XIV, No. 3), 1958.

demands, as defined in our study, were requirements to accept responsibilities. Thus, children who were exposed to high demands would be expected to have a relatively clear perception of (and probably considerable practice in) adult role responsibilities.

High demands did not bear this negative relationship to criminality:

DEMANDS AND TYPES OF DEVIANCE

	Per Cent Who Became Alcoholics	Per Cent Who Became Criminals
High demands (N: 60)	3	17
Moderate demands (N: 108) ...	17	15
Low demands (N: 62)	15	29

High criminal rates were, however, significantly related to low demands ($P < .02$).[22] That is, criminality did appear among families in which the parents either were willing to perform the child's tasks for him or took no interest in the child's behavior. (On the basis of the findings reported in the previous section, we believe the latter group would be the ones whose sons became criminals.)

4. A significantly lower proportion of alcoholics were second-generation Americans. Although we have no direct evidence to support the hypothesis, we are inclined to believe that immigrants would tend to have relatively high and clearly defined expectations for their sons. Immigrants frequently expect their sons to "complete" the process of "Americanization" and to take advantage of the relatively open class system. We found that criminality was not significantly related to parental immigration.

5. A significantly lower proportion of alcoholics had strongly Catholic mothers. Again, we have no direct evidence to support our belief, yet we think it likely that Catholicism provides standards of behavior that would tend to supplement those of the family in the specification of adult roles. We are, of course, assuming that strongly Catholic women would be likely to raise their children in that faith. Religion was not significantly related to criminality.

Thus, we found that experiences which would seem to lead to inadequate perception of the male role were significantly related only to alcoholism, and not to criminality.

Imitation of a Deviant Model and Criminality

Alcoholism seems to be at least partially a result of inadequate role specification; alcoholics apparently fail to develop clear self-concepts. On the other hand, criminality appears to be influenced by the boy's imitation of a criminal or aggressive paternal model.

Perhaps one reason for this difference can be found in the deviance rates as they reflect the "power structure" of the family:

PARENTAL DOMINANCE AND TYPE OF DEVIANCE

	Per Cent Who Became Alcoholics	Per Cent Who Became Criminals
Father dominant (N: 78)	9	27
Mother dominant (N: 75)	16	13
Equal dominance (N: 18)	11	11

Among families in which the fathers were dominant, the sons were significantly more likely to become criminals than alcoholics ($P < .05$).[23] Neither alcoholics nor criminals differed significantly from nondeviants in the power structure of their families. Therefore, paternal dominance does not appear to be a *cause* of criminality, but, rather, a factor that tends to mediate against alcoholism, given the conditions that promote deviance.

Except for paternal antagonism and escapism, we found that the father seems to play a relatively insignificant part in the production of alcoholism. Alcoholism of the son, we have seen, was not significantly related to paternal alcoholism or deviance.* Criminality, on the other hand, was strongly related to having a criminal or a deviant role model ($P < .001$):[24]

PATERNAL ROLE MODEL AND TYPE OF DEVIANCE

Paternal Model	Per Cent Who Became Alcoholics	Per Cent Who Became Criminals
Criminal (N: 40)	20	35
Deviant, noncriminal (N: 63) ...	11	24
Nondeviant (N: 116)	9	11

* Fathers who were alcoholic, criminal, or blatantly promiscuous were considered as deviant. Alcoholism of the son was significantly related to criminality of the father, but there seems to be no reason to attribute this to identification with the father.

It is known that paternal rejection, too, is related to criminality. The importance of both paternal deviance and rejection in producing a criminal as compared to their relative unimportance in producing an alcoholic can be seen in the table below:

PATERNAL ATTITUDE TOWARD BOY, ROLE MODEL,
AND TYPE OF DEVIANCE

	Per Cent Who Became Alcoholics	Per Cent Who Became Criminals
Affectionate father		
Nondeviant (N: 74)	11	5
Deviant (N: 42)	10	31
Rejecting father		
Nondeviant (N: 30)	10	27
Deviant (N: 46)	17	33

Clearly, paternal rejection was strongly related to crime: among the nondeviant fathers, crime rates were significantly higher for those who rejected their sons $(P < .01)$.[25]

Yet imitation of a deviant model seems to be an equally important factor in the production of criminal behavior. An affectionate deviant father was significantly more likely to have a criminal son than was an affectionate nondeviant father $(P < .001)$.[26] Furthermore, if the father was affectionate, paternal deviance was significantly more likely to lead to criminality than to alcoholism $(P < .025)$.[27]

Thus, whereas the nature of the paternal model seems to be unrelated to alcoholism, it seems to be strongly related to criminality.

Summary: Role Specification and Type of Deviance

Alcoholism, unlike criminality, seems to be partially a product of role confusion. The alcoholics differed from the nondeviants in that they more frequently had been subjected to conflicting demands and had fathers who were escapists. They were seldom subjected to high demands; only a few were sons of immigrants or of Catholic mothers.

On the other hand, criminality, unlike alcoholism, seems to stem partially from imitation of a deviant model and partially from response to paternal rejection. A significantly higher proportion of the criminals than of the nondeviants had deviant fathers and were rejected by their fathers.

Here we have the proportions of alcoholics,* of criminals, and of nondeviants who had experienced each of these backgrounds:

ROLE SPECIFICATION AND TYPE OF DEVIANCE

(*Subjects about whom there was no information were omitted*)

Background	Per Cent of Alcoholics	Per Cent of Nonalcoholic Criminals	Per Cent of Nondeviants
Counterinfluence in family	(N: 29) 24[a]	(N: 44) 5	(N: 158) 4[a]
Paternal escapism	(N: 21) 67[a]	(N: 38) 53	(N: 104) 40[a]
High demands	(N: 29) 7[a]	(N: 44) 23	(N: 157) 30[a]
Immigrant father	(N: 28) 32[a]	(N: 42) 48	(N: 156) 54[a]
Strongly Catholic mother	(N: 29) 7[a]	(N: 43) 21	(N: 153) 29[a]
Father dominant	(N: 21) 33[a]	(N: 33) 64[a]	(N: 128) 47
Alcoholic father[c]	(N: 26) 42	(N: 42) 52[a]	(N: 151) 26[a]
Criminal father[c]	(N: 26) 31[b]	(N: 42) 33[a]	(N: 151) 12[a,b]
If father affectionate, deviant	(N: 12) 33[b]	(N: 17) 76[a,b]	(N: 87) 29[a]
If father nondeviant, rejecting	(N: 11) 27	(N: 12) 67[a]	(N: 81) 23[a]

[a] Significant differences are noted, the superior [a] marking the two groups compared.

[b] These differences also were significant.

[c] The twenty-one fathers who were both criminals and alcoholics were included in both categories for separate comparisons.

On the basis of this information, it seems fair to conclude that role confusion differentiates alcoholics not only from nondeviants but also from criminals.

CHANNELING FACTORS: AN AGGRESSIVE ENVIRONMENT

Some theories of alcoholism suggest that addiction to alcohol is a form of self-aggression. We found no causal evidence to support this view. Many of the measures we used for describing child-rearing techniques were designed to test the possibility of heightened aggressiveness in our subjects. These variables were not significantly related to alcoholism although their importance in the backgrounds of criminals was clearly indicated. The criminal alcoholics, unlike the noncriminal alcoholics, tended to have backgrounds conducive to heightened aggressiveness.

* The criminal and the noncriminal alcoholics do not differ significantly with respect to any of these variables.

Several measures were used. Three were clearly based on an assumption that an aggressive paternal model would tend to heighten aggressiveness. A variety of measures indicated that criminality was a response to an aggressive model: Forty fathers directly and with little restraint expressed their aggressive feelings in the presence of their children; 35 per cent of their sons became criminals (P < .005).[28] Twenty-seven fathers assumed the role of "dictator" in family affairs; 41 per cent of their sons became criminals (P < .005).[29] One hundred eighteen fathers used physically punitive discipline; 29 per cent of their sons became criminals (P < .005).[30]

Still other measures of aggressiveness in the environment not only distinguished the criminals from the nondeviants but also differentiated the criminal alcoholics from the noncriminal alcoholics.*

From the observations made of parental behavior, we had classified the discipline of each parent as "punitive" (use of physical punishment, e.g., severe beatings) or nonpunitive (absence of physical punishment). Punitive discipline by the father, though strongly related to criminality, was related to alcoholism only if he was the major disciplinarian. When we compared the alcoholics to the nondeviants, we found a negative relationship between alcoholism and the use of punitive discipline by the mother. On the other hand, when we compared the criminals to the nondeviants, we found that maternal punitiveness was significantly related to criminality (P < .005).[31] Thus we can assume that the mother's use of physical punishment tends to heighten aggressiveness, which leads to crime.

Realizing that an important feature in the backgrounds of alcoholics consists in their apparent rejection of their fathers, one would expect that the mother's punitiveness would have a stronger effect than the father's punitiveness in heightening aggressiveness among alcoholics.

Again, it should be emphasized that we found no reason to believe that heightened aggressiveness is related to alcoholism; yet we did find that the alcoholic criminals differed from the alcoholic noncriminals in the amount of aggression apparent in their

* For these latter comparisons, because of the small number of cases, we used the Fisher-Yates test, one-tailed.

environment: a significantly higher proportion of alcoholic criminals than of alcoholic noncriminals had mothers who used punitive discipline (P < .05).[32]

As a second check on the relationship between an aggressive environment and deviance, we looked at the sixty-four subjects who had been punitively disciplined by *both* parents: 38 per cent had become nonalcoholic criminals, 11 per cent had become alcoholic criminals, but none were noncriminal alcoholics. A significantly higher proportion of the nonalcoholic criminals than of the nondeviants had been subjected to punitive discipline by both parents (P < .001).[33] Also, by using this measure of environmental aggressiveness, we found that the criminal alcoholics differed significantly from the noncriminal alcoholics (P < .025).[34]

It seems, therefore, as though an aggressive environment was strongly conducive to criminality. If it exists concurrently with heightened dependency conflict and role confusion, a combination of alcoholism and criminality was likely to result; in the absence of dependency conflict or role confusion, a nonalcoholic but criminal personality tended to be developed.

Similarly, we found verbal aggression to be related to criminality. We had rated the extent to which the child was subjected to threats. For this latter classification, we considered only the threats themselves, not whether they were fulfilled; threats of severe beatings, of castration, of desertion, are examples of what we considered "extreme use of threats" if they were made with regularity. The parents of 104 boys had used extreme threats in attempting to control the child; thirty-four of these boys became nonalcoholic criminals, nine became alcoholic criminals, and three became noncriminal alcoholics.

A comparison of nonalcoholic criminals to nondeviants revealed that extreme use of threats was significantly related to criminality (P < .001).[35] In comparing the criminal alcoholics to the noncriminal alcoholics, we found only a nonsignificant tendency for this form of aggression to differentiate the two groups.

Punitive discipline and use of threats may be considered as two different forms (nonverbal and verbal) of the direct expression of aggression. We hoped to obtain a fuller measure of indirect aggression by examining parental comparisons of the boy to other children. Many of our subjects were rarely compared to others; for others, comparisons that were made alternated between being favorable and unfavorable. Yet 116 boys were frequently compared to others in a consistent fashion. For sixty-nine boys, these comparisons were generally unfavorable; 22 per cent became nonalcoholic criminals, 12 per cent became alcoholic criminals, and only 1 per cent became noncriminal alcoholics. Unfavorable comparisons, we found, were significantly related to criminality (P < .05).[36] Also, among alcoholics, the criminals had been more frequently subjected to this form of aggression (P < .05).[37]

These analyses have indicated the importance of an aggressive environment in the channeling of deviance. The proportions of noncriminal alcoholics, of criminal alcoholics, of nonalcoholic criminals, and of nondeviants who had experienced each of these forms of aggression are shown in the following table.

AGGRESSIVE ENVIRONMENT AND TYPE OF DEVIANCE

(Subjects about whom there was no information were omitted)

Background	Per Cent of Noncriminal Alcoholics	Per Cent of Criminal Alcoholics	Per Cent of Nonalcoholic Criminals	Per Cent of Nondeviants
Unrestrained paternal aggressiveness.	(N: 9) 11	(N: 15) 33	(N: 38) 37[a]	(N: 137) 15[a]
Father a "dictator"......	(N: 8) 13	(N: 13) 24	(N: 34) 32[a]	(N: 127) 9[a]
Punitive discipline used by father	(N: 9) 56	(N: 14) 71	(N: 41) 83[a]	(N: 124) 56[a]
Punitive discipline used by mother	(N: 10) 20[a]	(N: 18) 61[a]	(N: 43) 70[a]	(N: 152) 45[a]
Punitive discipline used by both parents	(N: 8) 0[a]	(N: 14) 50[a]	(N: 40) 60[a]	(N: 133) 25[a]
Extreme use of threats	(N: 10) 30	(N: 14) 64	(N: 40) 85[a]	(N: 128) 45[a]
Unfavorable comparisons made about boy	(N: 5) 20[a]	(N: 10) 80[a]	(N: 19) 79[a]	(N: 82) 55[a]

[a] The differences were significant. Nonalcoholic criminals were compared to nondeviants; alcoholic criminals were compared to noncriminal alcoholics.

Aggression in the environment appeared to be consistently related to deviance. Because none of these forms of aggression appeared significantly more frequently in the backgrounds of noncriminal alcoholics than of nondeviants, we would tend to conclude that an aggressive environment does not lead directly to alcoholism. Because all of these influences appear significantly more frequently in the backgrounds of nonalcoholic criminals than of nondeviants, we would conclude that an aggressive environment is an important causal factor of criminality. And because many of these measures of aggression in the environment differentiate the criminal alcoholics from the noncriminal alcoholics (while measures of dependency and role specification do not) it seems apparent that the two "types" of alcoholics differ primarily in their level of aggression.

CHANNELING FACTORS: SOCIAL CORRELATES

In previous chapters, we have noted certain sociological distinctions between the alcoholics and the nondeviants. In addition to the causal differences we have discussed, we found that various social correlates tended to distinguish the alcoholics not only from nondeviants but also from nonalcoholic criminals.

One of the primary sociological distinctions among types of deviants relates to social class. By defining as "middle class" the families in which the father held a professional or a white-collar job or had received a high school diploma, we found that the majority of criminals had lower-class backgrounds. Alcoholics, significantly more frequently than criminals, were from the middle class (P < .05).[38] Also, the criminal alcoholics came from middle-class backgrounds significantly less frequently than the noncriminal alcoholics (P < .02).[39]

The type of neighborhood in which a child was reared appeared also to influence the type of deviance. Criminals, during childhood, had been exposed to the disorganization of transitional neighborhoods significantly more frequently than nondeviants (P < .05)[40] or than alcoholics (P < .02).[41]

Thus, the criminal alcoholics differed from the noncriminal alcoholics in social class: the criminal alcoholic was less likely to have a middle-class background; the alcoholics were also less likely to have been reared in transitional neighborhoods than were nonalcoholic criminals, who tended to have been residents in transitional neighborhoods during childhood.

SOCIAL CORRELATES AND TYPE OF DEVIANCE
(Subjects for whom there was no information were omitted)

	Per Cent of Noncriminal Alcoholics	Per Cent of Criminal Alcoholics	Per Cent of Nonalcoholic Criminals	Per Cent of Nondeviants
Middle class	(N: 9) 67	(N: 16) 13	(N: 38) 8	(N: 139) 19
Transitional neighborhood ..	(N: 10) 30	(N: 18) 61	(N: 44) 77	(N: 157) 60

SUMMARY

In this chapter we have focused upon two prevalent types of social deviance: alcoholism and criminality. Both forms of deviance share certain characteristics: both, to a large extent, appear to be by-products of American society, for the United States ranks highest in the Western world in criminal rates and ties with Sweden for the highest rate of alcoholism; both occur primarily among the male population; both are essentially destructive forms of behavior—although alcoholism may be considered primarily self-destructive and criminality is more directly aimed at the destruction of others or their property, each results in self-destruction and loss to others. Yet, why, within American society, do some men become alcoholics rather than criminals?

The backgrounds of both alcoholics and criminals contained conditions which, it may be assumed, would result in general instability. These might be considered "stress conditions":

The parents of alcoholics and criminals exhibited intense conflict significantly more frequently than did the parents of nondeviants.

Incest or illegitimacy occurred significantly more frequently among the families of alcoholics and criminals than among the families of nondeviants.

A significantly higher proportion of the mothers of alcoholics and of criminals than of nondeviants held ambiguous family roles, and were criminals, alcoholics, or blatantly promiscuous.

Both the alcoholics and the nonalcoholic criminals were emotionally frustrated in childhood. Yet the alcoholics differed from the criminals in the nature of this frustration.

Whereas the backgrounds of alcoholics most likely gave rise to dependency conflict, the backgrounds of criminals most likely extinguished dependency desires. This conclusion was based on the following differences:

Maternal ambivalence and escapism were significantly related to alcoholism; maternal rejection was significantly related to criminality.

Absence of maternal affection resulted in alcoholism if the father was present in the home; criminality, if the father was absent.

When the attitudes of both parents toward their son were taken into account, we found that alcoholism occurred most frequently with the combination of some maternal affection and overt rejection (by either the father or the mother); criminality occurred most frequently among sons of women who were consistently unaffectionate.

Punitive maternal discipline resulted in high criminal rates and relatively low alcoholism rates. Maternal punitiveness was significantly more likely to lead to crime than to alcoholism.

Parental antagonism was particularly productive of alcoholism; an attitude of indifference between the parents was more productive of criminality.

The alcoholics, unlike the criminals, had backgrounds that would contribute to role confusion. The following findings support the view that alcoholics have failed to develop a consistent self-concept:

A significantly lower proportion of the alcoholics than of the non-deviants had high demands imposed on them during childhood. The absence of high demands was not related to criminality.

A significantly higher proportion of the alcoholics than of the non-deviants had fathers who, when faced with a crisis, reacted by implicit or explicit escape. The fathers of criminals tended to respond un-realistically to crises, yet escapism was not their primary reaction.

A significantly lower proportion of the alcoholics than of the non-deviants were second-generation Americans, whose families could be expected to have more clearly specified expectations for their sons. The father's birthplace was not related to criminality.

A significantly lower proportion of the alcoholics than of the non-deviants had strongly Catholic maternal backgrounds. Religion was not related to criminality.

A significantly lower proportion of alcoholics than of criminals had fathers who took a dominant role in family decisions.

Although we do not maintain that imitation of a deviant paternal model is *the* primary cause of criminality,[42] we believe that paternal deviance is clearly more influential to the development of criminality than to the development of alcoholism:

Paternal alcoholism was not significantly related to the son's alcoholism, yet paternal criminality was significantly related to criminality.

Affectionate but deviant fathers significantly more frequently had criminal sons than did affectionate nondeviant fathers.

Among men whose fathers had been affectionate, those whose fathers were deviant more often became criminals than alcoholics.

Heightened aggression, not surprisingly, was found to be closely related to criminality. We found no evidence, however, that heightened aggression was causally linked with alcoholism.

Criminals had aggressive paternal models. A significantly greater proportion of criminals than of nondeviants had highly aggressive fathers. Paternal aggressiveness was not related to alcoholism.

A significantly greater proportion of the criminals than of the nondeviants had fathers whose power in the family approximated that of a "dictator." This dictatorial character of the paternal role was not related to alcoholism.

A significantly greater proportion of the criminals than of the nondeviants had been subjected to punitive discipline by the father. Paternal punitiveness, as such, was not related to alcoholism.

A significantly greater proportion of criminals than of nondeviants had been subjected to punitive discipline by their mothers. Yet maternal punitiveness had no tendency to lead to noncriminal alcoholism.

A significantly higher proportion of the criminals than of the nondeviants had been subjected to punitive discipline by both parents. This highly punitive atmosphere was not related to alcoholism.

A significantly higher proportion of the parents of criminals than of nondeviants had used severe threats in their attempts to control their sons. This form of aggression was not related to alcoholism.

A significantly higher proportion of the criminals than of the nondeviants had been compared unfavorably to other children. These unfavorable comparsions were not related to alcoholism.

Besides differentiating the nonalcoholic criminal from the nondeviant, heightened aggressiveness seems to be the primary distinction between criminal alcoholics hand noncriminal alcoholics:

A significantly higher proportion of the alcoholics whose mothers used punitive discipline had criminal records.

A significantly higher proportion of the criminal alcoholics as compared to the noncriminal alcoholics had been subject to punitive discipline from both parents.

A significantly higher proportion of the criminal than of the non-criminal alcoholics had been compared unfavorably to other children.

Two socioeconomic factors seemed to channel deviance:

Alcoholics, significantly more frequently than criminals, came from the middle class.

Alcoholics, significantly less frequently than nonalcoholic criminals, had lived in transitional neighborhoods during childhood.

Criminal alcoholics, significantly more frequently than noncriminal alcoholics, were from the lower class.

Nonalcoholic criminals, significantly more frequently than nondeviants, had been reared in transitional neighborhoods.

More briefly, one might chart the origins of alcoholism and criminality as follows:

	Noncriminal Alcoholics	Criminal Alcoholics	Nonalcoholic Criminals
General stress	present	present	present
Dependency conflict	present	present	absent
Emotional coldness	absent	absent	present
Inadequate self-concept	present	present	absent
Imitation of deviant paternal model	absent	absent	present
Heightened aggression	absent	present	present
Middle-class values	present	absent	absent

Thus, this comparative analysis points to the similarities and differences among three types of deviants: the noncriminal alcoholics, the criminal alcoholics, and the nonalcoholic criminals. All three had backgrounds conducive to general anxiety. The family environments of alcoholics, both criminal and noncriminal, tended to heighten dependency conflict. The family environments of non-alcoholic criminals, on the other hand, were typified by extreme emotional coldness. Whereas the alcoholics (criminal and non-criminal) were subjected to influences leading to inadequate role perception, the behavior of the nonalcoholic criminals tended to reflect the behavior of their paternal models. Finally, two similarities of background tended to link the alcoholic to the non-alcoholic criminals and to differentiate both from the noncriminals: The criminals had been subjected to overt or covert aggressions, and they more often came from lower-class backgrounds.[43]

8

THE PERSONALITY OF ALCOHOLICS

/Latent homosexuality, oral fixation, introversion, extroversion, a desire for omnipotence, feelings of inferiority, suppressed or expressed aggressiveness—these and many other traits have been attributed to alcoholics./ Lists of characteristics drawn from one piece of research or one theory have often been contradicted by other studies. Thus, Carney Landis, after reviewing the research up to 1945, felt forced to conclude: "Most of the theories of the alcoholic personality are based on a minimum of factual evidence. Such evidence as does exist is seldom clear-cut or definitive. Hence, the theories are often contradictory."[1]

In 1957, after analyzing the research on personality, Leonard Syme discouragingly reported: "There is no warrant for concluding that persons of one type are more likely to become alcoholics than another type."[2]

In 1958, John D. Armstrong pulled together a variety of contemporary studies and found the process to be like "chasing the will-o'-the-wisp." "The quest for an alcoholic personality or constellation of frequently predominant characteristics in alcoholism has barely begun," he wrote.[3]

/This search for the basic alcoholic personality has been seriously hindered by the fact that it has been impossible to separate the personality characteristics that may be a *result* of addiction from those that may be a *cause* of, or at least precede, alcoholism./ Armstrong's comment on this problem is pertinent:

One of the most vexing aspects of the situation is the clinical experience of watching changes in personality take place as a disease situation advances, leaving one in almost complete bewilderment as to what picture existed before the superimposition of a pattern of attitude and behavior which we recognize as alcoholic.

There is no report of studies in which it was possible successfully to examine the premorbid or even the early alcoholic history in such a way that a reliable personality profile could be obtained and compared with that observed in the fully developed diseased state.[4]

In our study we dissociated the prealcoholic from the post-alcoholic personality. Since our information was gathered in childhood, we could record descriptions of the subjects before they became alcoholic. Because a substantial number of the subjects' fathers were addicted to alcohol and were studied in their day-to-day behavior, we could also simultaneously examine the characteristics of postalcoholics. Consequently, one can specify what syndromes of personality preceded the disorder and what characteristics appear to be precipitated by alcoholism.

First, let us examine the sample of adult alcoholics.

THE PERSONALITY OF MALE ALCOHOLICS IN ADULTHOOD

Eighty-three fathers in the study were defined as alcoholics;* that is, their repeated drinking at some time prior to 1945 had interfered with their interpersonal relations or their social or economic functioning. Twenty-three of the men had not been arrested for drunkenness and ten had been arrested only once. These men had been classified as alcoholics because they had lost their jobs due to excessive drinking or had received medical treatment specifically for alcoholism, or because marital unhappiness was attributable primarily to their excessive drinking. Five of the alcoholics had been classified as alcoholics solely because they had been arrested at least twice for drunkenness. The majority, forty-five, of the alcoholic fathers were considered alcoholics by both criteria.

Since the men were observed in their routine activities, the methodological defects ordinarily found in studies of persons con-

* This figure includes the fathers of men arrested once for drunkenness, and thus is larger than the sample used in previous analyses.

fined in institutions (jails, sanatoriums, mental hospitals) do not
affect this analysis. When compared to a sample of nondeviant
fathers (neither alcoholic nor criminal), a number of significant
differences became apparent.

The Relation of Adult Alcoholics to Society

/It is hardly surprising to note that the alcoholics were social
outcasts. They found it extremely difficult to hold regular jobs,
and economically they failed to provide for their families./ Although the depression hit most of the families in our study, significantly fewer alcoholics than nondeviants were able to find work
on a regular basis (P < .001).[5]

EMPLOYMENT OF ADULT ALCOHOLICS AND NONDEVIANTS

	Per Cent of Alcoholics (N: 82)	Per Cent of Nondeviants (N: 105)
Regularly employed	23	58
Irregularly employed	67	33
Regularly unemployed	10	9

/One would also expect that alcoholics, in addition to being
economically unstable, would also be less actively involved in community organizations. /To test this belief, we examined the social
activities of the subjects. These were of two types: "informal" participation included social gatherings (e.g., parties, poker games)
that did not involve official "membership rites"; "formal" participation included any group with "membership rites" (e.g., the
P.T.A., saloon clubs, neighborhood organizations, the Cambridge
Civic Association). /The alcoholics, quite naturally, tended to
avoid involvement in formal community organizations/(P < .02).[6]

PARTICIPATION IN COMMUNITY GROUPS OF ADULT ALCOHOLICS AND NONDEVIANTS

	Per Cent of Alcoholics (N: 57)	Per Cent of Nondeviants (N: 89)
Little or no participation	56	43
Participation only in informal groups	40	36
Participation in formal groups	4	21

/ Thus, as one would expect, the adult alcoholics were both economically and socially less stable than their nondeviant counterparts. /

The Relation of Adult Alcoholics to Their Families

How do alcoholics interact with their families? The answer to this question is not so immediately furnished by common sense. Would alcoholics be likely to reject their sons or turn to their children as a source of affection? Would alcoholics tend to dominate their families or, because of the incapacities caused by their disorder, tend to take a passive role? To find the answer to these and other issues, we analyzed the alcoholics' relations to their families.

/ The alcoholics were much more likely to reject their children and much less prone to demonstrate their affection in an active manner / (P < .001).[7]

THE ATTITUDES OF ADULT ALCOHOLICS AND NONDEVIANTS TOWARD THEIR SONS

	Per Cent of Alcoholics (N: 72)	Per Cent of Nondeviants (N: 97)
Actively affectionate	17	43
Passively affectionate	30	33
Alternating	10	6
Passively rejecting	22	11
Actively rejecting	21	7

It is difficult to know why an alcoholic rejects his son. We would guess (on the basis of the causal evidence previously presented) that the typical alcoholic is unsure of receiving love from other people; he may also be very unsure of how to give love. The result might often be hesitation to make affectionate overtures to his family.

The alcoholics also differed from the nondeviant adults in the type of roles they assumed in the family. The fathers in the study could be categorized into four groups. The "dictators" were those who completely dominated their families and made almost every decision. The "leaders" were men who gave general guidance to family affairs but were flexible in bowing to reasonable arguments from other members of the family. The "passive" fathers, on the other hand, abdicated family responsibility to the wife or one of the elder sons. Alcoholics clearly tended not to be "leaders," but tended to play a passive, dependent role in their families (P < .001).[8] We found, too, that among the more dominant males, the alcoholics were significantly more likely to be dictators than leaders (P < .001):[9]

The Familial Roles of Adult Alcoholics and Nondeviants

	Per Cent of Alcoholics (N: 64)	Per Cent of Nondeviants (N: 95)
Dictator	19	10
Leader	23	63
Passive	58	27

Not surprisingly, we found a high degree of intense conflict between husband and wife. The majority of the alcoholics' families were rent with dissension; only a tiny minority of the nondeviants' homes, on the other hand, suffered intense conflict (P < .001):[10]

Parental Conflict in the Homes of Adult Alcoholics and Nondeviants

	Per Cent of Alcoholics (N: 74)	Per Cent of Nondeviants (N: 91)
No conflict	8	58
Some conflict	32	35
Intense conflict	60	7

Intense parental conflict was related to alcoholism in the children; thus, this seems to be one more factor leading to the high rate of deviance found in the descendants of inebriates.

The alcoholics varied from the nondeviants in the ways they disciplined their children. The fathers in the study were divided according to how they controlled their sons. Some fathers disciplined in a "consistently punitive" fashion; the son knew that if he committed a certain act, his father would respond with physical punishment. Other fathers were equally consistent, but did not use physical methods. These men depended on reasoning and withdrawing privileges or love as their means of controlling the child. We described these men as "consistently nonpunitive."

Other fathers varied in their demands. At times, they would punish a certain act (for example, staying out in the street beyond a curfew); at other times, however, they would ignore the same action or even condone it. These inconsistent fathers were divided into two groups: "erratically punitive" and "erratically nonpunitive," depending on the form of discipline.

A fifth group of men simply did not care about their child's activities and imposed no discipline of any sort. These we put under the category of "lax" disciplinarians.

A comparison of the alcoholic and the nondeviant fathers revealed that alcoholics were much more likely to be erratically punitive or lax in controlling their sons (P < .005):[11]

DISCIPLINARY METHODS OF ADULT ALCOHOLICS AND NONDEVIANTS

	Per Cent of Alcoholics (N: 68)	Per Cent of Nondeviants (N: 87)
Consistently punitive	16	26
Consistently nonpunitive	10	30
Erratically punitive	50	30
Erratically nonpunitive	8	6
Lax	16	8

Again, this fact bodes ill for the future of alcoholics' sons, for we have demonstrated that the two forms of discipline more often found in the alcoholics' families—erratic punitiveness and laxity—are significantly involved in causing crime.[12]

It would appear, therefore, that alcoholics are unstable members of their families as well as of their communities. They perform their roles as fathers in a passive or dictatorial manner; they are prone to express their various frustrations through conflict with their wives, rejection of their sons, and the imposition of erratically punitive discipline on their children. Thus, it seems, people who are forced to live with alcoholics are doomed to an unhappy existence.

The Personality of Adult Alcoholics

What is the alcoholic's view of his society? What values does he uphold? What intrapersonal traits differentiate him from the nonalcoholic? To answer these questions, we analyzed certain aspects of the alcoholic syndrome.

The alcoholics differed strikingly from the nondeviants in their view of the world. Many of the subjects in the study faced the world with, at least, a façade of self-confidence. Other men felt themselves to be unjustly victimized by society; they tended to be self-pitying men who felt that they had been double-crossed or given a raw deal. Although a majority of the nondeviants acted in a self-confident way, a majority of the alcoholics thought that they were victims of an unfair society (P < .001):[13]

THE VIEW OF SOCIETY OF ADULT ALCOHOLICS AND OF NONDEVIANTS

	Per Cent of Alcoholics (N: 64)	Per Cent of Nondeviants (N: 93)
Self-confident	19	52
Neutral	22	26
Victimized	59	22

This feeling of victimization may reflect a need for self-justification on the part of alcoholics. Another trait of adult alcoholics, "feelings of grandiosity," may be related to this same need.

One might expect that the alcoholics would compensate for their inadequacies by inflating their self-image. Indeed, the alcoholics were more likely to exhibit feelings of "grandiosity"— inflated estimates of their abilities and virtues (P < .005):[14]

FEELINGS OF GRANDIOSITY IN ADULT ALCOHOLICS AND NONDEVIANTS

	Per Cent of Alcoholics (N: 61)	Per Cent of Nondeviants (N: 89)
No apparent feelings of grandiosity	64	84
Feelings of grandiosity present	36	16

In addition to these more specific attitudes, we classified the general "value orientations" of the men in the study. The detailed records indicated numerous situations about which the subjects had to make choices; the primary basis for their choices was classified as being one of five types: (1) *security*—a desire to avoid risk, to maintain or obtain physical security; (2) *popularity*—a desire to be liked by others; (3) *achievement*—a desire to do something well; (4) *status*—a desire to be respected (although not necessarily liked) by others, to be thought better than most people; and (5) *enjoyment*—a desire for immediate sensual stimulation.

The nondeviants were much more likely to place security or status as highest in their scale of values, while the alcoholics tended to seek immediate enjoyment above all else (P < .001).*[15]

THE PRIMARY VALUES OF ADULT ALCOHOLICS AND OF NONDEVIANTS

	Per Cent of Alcoholics (N: 65)	Per Cent of Nondeviants (N: 88)
Security	30	62
Popularity	0	1
Achievement	0	9
Status	5	18
Enjoyment	65	10

"Enjoyment" as a value emphasis, in contrast to security, popularity, achievement, or status, involves no deferment of reward. Thus, the alcoholics appeared to be less strongly inhibited.

This lack of inhibition is seen in another trait differentiating the adult alcoholics from the nondeviants: unrestrained aggressiveness. Their aggressive behavior was classified into three divisions. Some were "highly inhibited"; to the observers' knowledge they never were openly hostile or angry. Many were "moderately aggressive"; they expressed feelings of irritation through "normal" channels—that is, through the forms of behavior sanctioned by our culture. Another group were "aggressively unrestrained"; their

---

* Closely related to a person's values is his "conscience orientation." In a recent article ("A Tentative Theory of Conscience" in *Decisions, Values, and Groups*, edited by Dorothy Willmer, Pergamon Press, New York, 1960), we outlined four basic types of conscience: the other-directed (anxiety about relations to others), the authoritarian (anxiety about status), the integral (anxiety about maintaining a consistent self-image), and the hedonist (anxiety concerning repressen dependency). In passing, it should be noted that the majority (52 per cent) of the nondeviants were authoritarian, while close to a majority of the alcoholics (44 per cent) were hedonistic (X^2 34.57, d.f. 3).

expressions of anger often exceeded the bounds imposed by society. Although only a very few of the nondeviants were intensely aggressive, more than a third of the alcoholics had been classified as extremely aggressive (P < .001).[16]

AGGRESSION IN ADULT ALCOHOLICS AND NONDEVIANTS

	Per Cent of Alcoholics (N: 73)	Per Cent of Nondeviants (N: 92)
Strongly inhibited aggression	9	11
Moderate aggression	55	86
Unrestrained aggression	36	3

In addition to being relatively more aggressive, the alcoholics tended to exhibit markedly dependent behavior in an open fashion. Dependent behavior in a man—overt seeking for comfort, care, and direct guidance—is highly disapproved in American culture. Yet a small proportion of males in the study did exhibit this type of behavior. At the opposite extreme, some subjects could be described as "highly masculine"—they sought to appear especially strong, resolute, courageous, and responsible. Alcoholics were significantly more likely to exhibit openly dependent behavior than were the nondeviants (P < .005).[17]

DEPENDENT BEHAVIOR IN ADULT ALCOHOLICS AND NONDEVIANTS

	Per Cent of Alcoholics (N: 74)	Per Cent of Nondeviants (N: 98)
Highly masculine	11	20
Normally masculine	69	74
Dependent	20	6

Thus, the adult alcoholic's personality contains contrasts that distinguish him from the nondeviant. Adult alcoholics may be depicted as lacking self-confidence, but entertaining inflated ideas of their own importance; as exhibiting markedly dependent behavior, but alienating others through overt aggression.

The Traits of Adult Alcoholics

This analysis, based on direct and extended observations, has revealed that adult alcoholics differed from nondeviants in a number of significant ways.

In relation to their society, alcoholics were significantly more likely to have been irregularly employed (P < .001); and not participated in formal community organizations (P < .02).

In relation to their families, alcoholics were significantly more likely to have rejected their sons (P < .001); played a passive role in their families or to have been "dictators" (P < .001); been in intense conflict with their family (P < .001); and disciplined their sons in an erratically punitive or lax manner (P < .005).

In terms of personal "traits," alcoholics were significantly more likely to have felt victimized by an unjust society (P < .001); shown feelings of grandiosity (P < .005); valued enjoyment above all else (P < .001); been intensely aggressive (P < .001); and been openly dependent (P < .005).

These characteristics of adult alcoholics, we believe, tend to confirm the prominence of role confusion and dependency conflict as basic to the alcoholic personality.

This study is not unique in pointing to many of the traits we have mentioned; it does, however, differ from other studies in several respects: first, as we have mentioned, the analyses were based on direct observations of the adult alcoholics within their homes over an extensive period of time; second, the original observers did not know that any study of personality would be based on their reports; third, the reports were made by a variety of observers whose possible biases would tend to cancel one another; fourth, neither the original observers nor the raters focused on the problem of the alcoholic personality, and, thus, conscious theoretical biases were minimized; finally, the sample of alcoholics contains men who had never come to the attention of official agencies dealing with alcoholism. We have some confidence, therefore, that adult alcoholic men are truly distinguishable from adult nondeviant men in their relations to society and their families, and in their personalities.

Nevertheless, this study of adult alcoholics shares with other studies the disadvantage that the subjects were already alcoholics at the time of the observations. Many theories about the alcoholic personality presuppose that the characteristics of adult alcoholics are apparent prior to the onset of alcoholism. To test the validity of this supposition, we analyzed the twenty-nine boys who, in adulthood, manifested symptoms of alcoholism.

THE CHILDHOOD PERSONALITY OF PREALCOHOLICS

None of the subjects discussed in this section were known to be alcoholics at the time the observations were made (during childhood); nor were they known to be alcoholics by the raters who categorized their traits. As with the adult alcoholics, we shall discuss the relationships of the prealcoholics to their society and to their families, and then turn to their personalities.

The Relationship of Prealcoholics to Society

Unlike adult nondeviants, adult alcoholics, we have noted, tended to forgo group activities. The boys had been observed during work and play and then been classified by their group behavior: boys who generally played by themselves; boys who generally played with their peers, yet rarely led them; and boys who were frequently chosen (formally or informally) as leaders by their peers. We found that the prealcoholics did not differ significantly from the nondeviants:

GROUP PARTICIPATION OF ALCOHOLICS AND NONDEVIANTS
IN CHILDHOOD

	Per Cent of Alcoholics (N: 29)	Per Cent of Nondeviants (N: 158)
Seldom participates	10	15
Participates	76	72
Leads	14	13

Thus, the absence of group participation found among adult alcoholics was not manifested during childhood.

The Relationship of Prealcoholics to Their Families

We have noted the hostile attitude of adult alcoholics toward their families. Such men tended to reject their sons and fight with their wives. Family rejection was evident also among the prealcoholics.

Most of the children in the study indicated generally favorable attitudes toward their mothers. A smaller group of boys, however, expressed outright disapproval, disdain, or fear of their parents. The prealcoholics were significantly more likely to reject their mothers than were the nondeviants (P < .025).[18]

ATTITUDES TOWARD THE MOTHER OF ALCOHOLICS
AND NONDEVIANTS IN CHILDHOOD

	Per Cent of Alcoholics (N: 25)	Per Cent of Nondeviants (N: 143)
Favorable attitude	64	85
Unfavorable attitude	36	15

This relatively disapproving attitude of the alcoholics toward their mothers appears to have been somewhat independent of their mothers' attitudes toward them:

MOTHER'S ATTITUDE TOWARD BOY AND BOY'S ATTITUDE TOWARD
MOTHER AMONG ALCOHOLICS AND NONDEVIANTS IN CHILDHOOD

	Per Cent of Alcoholics with Unfavorable Attitudes toward Their Mothers		Per Cent of Nondeviants with Unfavorable Attitudes toward Their Mothers	
Mother affectionate	(N: 13)	15	(N: 111)	5
Mother alternating or rejecting	(N: 11)	64	(N: 31)	51

A higher proportion of the prealcoholic children (48 per cent) than of the nondeviants (31 per cent) also disapproved of their fathers; this difference was not, however, statistically significant.

In relation to their brothers and sisters, too, the potentially alcoholic children indicated a lack of affection for their families. Their attitudes toward their siblings were characterized by coolness and apparent indifference. While the nondeviant children tended more often to be companions of their siblings, the prealcoholic boys were more likely to appear totally indifferent $(P < .02)$.[19]

RELATION TO SIBLINGS OF ALCOHOLICS AND NONDEVIANTS
IN CHILDHOOD

	Per Cent of Alcoholics (N: 23)	Per Cent of Nondeviants (N: 124)
Indifferent	43	21
Competitive	9	10
Antagonistic	13	17
Companionable	35	52

Thus, the attitudes of the prealcoholics toward their parents and siblings seemed to presage the attitudes of the adult alcoholics toward their wives and children.

The Personality of Prealcoholics

Although the adult alcoholics lacked self-confidence, tending to feel victimized by society, we found no evidence of this trait among the prealcoholic boys.

"Self-confidence" in childhood had been categorized along a three-point continuum. The boys who demonstrated unusual fearlessness or faced difficult tasks without hesitation were considered "very self-confident." At the opposite extreme, we rated boys as exhibiting strong feelings of inferiority if they talked frequently of their lack of ability and their failures or if they were exceptionally hesitant about attempting even moderately difficult tasks because they feared failure. As we mentioned in Chapter 2, we discovered that the prealcoholic children had *less* frequently appeared to have strong inferiority feelings (P < .05).[20]

SELF-CONFIDENCE OF ALCOHOLICS AND NONDEVIANTS
IN CHILDHOOD

	Per Cent of Alcoholics (N: 29)	Per Cent of Nondeviants (N: 156)
Very self-confident	10	10
Moderately self-confident	80	58
Strong inferiority feelings	10	32

A further indication that the feeling of victimization was not evident in prealcoholics appeared when we analyzed the relation between "abnormal fears" during childhood and alcoholism. Some of the subjects felt great concern about unrealistic dangers; they often talked about fears of the dark, of "monsters," of being attacked. The potential alcoholics exhibited significantly *fewer* of these abnormal fears than did the nonalcoholics (P < .05).[21]

ABNORMAL FEARS OF ALCOHOLICS AND NONALCOHOLICS
IN CHILDHOOD

	Per Cent of Alcoholics (N: 25)	Per Cent of Nondeviants (N: 146)
Abnormal fears	28	50
No abnormal fears	72	50

We found, too, that the feelings of grandiosity among adult alcoholics were not markedly present among prealcoholics. Only a slightly higher proportion of the prealcoholics (36 per cent) than of the nondeviants (27 per cent) gave indications that they held inflated ideas of their own importance.

In another respect, however, we found that the prealcoholics resembled the adult alcoholics: a lack of inhibition in the area of aggression. We used a three-point scale to rate the aggressive behavior of the boys in the study. Boys who reacted to even slight frustrations with overt and exaggerated aggression, who fought constantly, were rated as extremely aggressive. At the other extreme, boys who almost never gave overt expression to hostility, regardless of provocation, were considered strongly inhibited.

The prealcoholic children had much more frequently exhibited unrestrained aggression and less frequently appeared to have been strongly inhibited (P < .02):[22]

AGGRESSIVE BEHAVIOR OF ALCOHOLICS AND NONDEVIANTS
IN CHILDHOOD

	Per Cent of Alcoholics (N: 28)	Per Cent of Nondeviants (N: 154)
Unrestrained aggression	36	12
Moderate aggression	50	56
Strongly inhibited aggression	14	32

In some cases, aggressive behavior manifested itself as sadism; a small proportion of boys exhibited this overtly destructive syndrome. Another group of boys were masochistic; they enjoyed playing games in which they were "victims," or in which they could receive pain. Although sadism was related to alcoholism, the prealcoholic boys did not more often indicate masochistic tendencies. Twenty-eight per cent of the prealcoholics and only 10 per cent of the nondeviants showed signs of sadism (P < .05).[23] Three per cent of the prealcoholics and 4 per cent of the nondeviants showed signs of masochism.

Self-aggression also failed to differentiate the prealcoholics from the nondeviants when the psychosomatic symptoms of acne, overweight, and stomach disorders were used as a measure of self-aggression; 10 per cent of the prealcoholics and 11 per cent of the nondeviants had these symptoms.

We have found that adult alcoholics were markedly dependent in their behavior. The attitudes of the prealcoholics toward their families suggest a tendency for them to deny dependency. Yet another characteristic of the prealcoholic—sex anxiety—might indicate the presence of dependency conflict. Although the differences are not statistically significant,[24] we found that a considerably higher proportion of the prealcoholics (54 per cent) than of the nondeviants (35 per cent) had been preoccupied with fears about sex.

Finally, we found that passive behavior among prealcoholics was negatively related to alcoholism (P < .05).[25] For this measure, we considered the physical activity of the subjects. The boys who had always to be moving or doing something were considered hyperactive. Other boys participated in activities, yet were able to sit quietly for reasonable periods of time. Still others remained inactive for exceptionally long periods of time, and were classified as passive.

ENERGY LEVEL OF ALCOHOLICS AND NONDEVIANTS
IN CHILDHOOD

	Per Cent of Alcoholics (N: 29)	Per Cent of Nondeviants (N: 155)
Hyperactive	31	21
Normally active	62	56
Passive	7	23

Thus, in the prealcoholics, we did not find the feelings of victimization or the absence of self-confidence that we noted among adult alcoholics. Nor did we find evidence that the prealcoholics had grandiosity feelings. Yet the prealcoholics, like the adult alcoholics, exhibited unrestrained aggressiveness. We found, too, that the prealcoholics tended to disapprove of their mothers, to be indifferent toward their siblings, to show signs of overt sex anxiety, and to have a tendency toward hyperactivity.

THE BASIC CHARACTERISTICS OF ALCOHOLICS

An examination of the character of prealcoholics in childhood has revealed a syndrome of personality traits that differentiate them from nonalcoholics. In this analysis, there was no possibility of retrospective bias; for the observations had been made when the subjects were children and had not yet become alcoholics and the categorizations were done by raters who did not know which subjects had become alcoholics.

This investigation has indicated that alcoholics in childhood were apparently self-contained. Compared to the nondeviants, the prealcoholics were more likely to have been[26] outwardly self-confident ($P < .05$); undisturbed by abnormal fears ($P < .05$); indifferent toward their siblings ($P < .02$); and disapproving of their mothers ($P < .025$).

The prealcoholics were also more aggressive and anxious. They tended more often to have been: highly aggressive ($P < .02$); sadistic ($P < .05$); and hyperactive ($P < .05$). There was no indication, however, of masochistic tendencies.

It is important to recognize that the sample of prealcoholics (observed in childhood) differed in several important ways from the sample of adult alcoholics: (1) The adult alcoholics tended to feel "victimized" by their society; the prealcoholics appeared to be self-confident. (2) The adult alcoholics were often highly dependent; the prealcoholics emphasized their independence. (3) Whereas the adult alcoholics tended to avoid group activities and to express feelings of grandiosity, we found neither of these traits distinguished the prealcoholic from the nonalcoholic children.

In certain other ways, the adult alcoholics resembled the prealcoholics—both groups were aggressive and both tended to reject members of their immediate families.

From these two sources of evidence, we can assume the existence of an "alcoholism-prone" character—a pattern of personality characteristics that is peculiarly sensitive to the attractions of alcohol. In childhood, the alcoholics exhibited several traits—apparent fearlessness, self-sufficiency, and aggressiveness—which, in our society, are generally regarded as being masculine. In terms of common cultural expectations, the potential alcoholics were very "manly," independent children; they accepted (and sometimes with a vengeance) the American stereotype of the male virtues.

Yet, for several reasons we would assume that this overemphasis on masculinity was a façade, covering up "feminine," dependent tendencies that were repugnant to the boys (and regarded as undesirable in American society).

First, we are aware that in adulthood the alcoholics often exhibited forms of dependent and passive behavior that are in direct contrast to the childhood façade. Unless we believe that alcoholism spontaneously created these traits, we can reasonably assume that traits like dependency and grandiosity and feelings of victimization were present in the prealcoholic's personality, but were—consciously or unconsciously—suppressed. By this interpretation, the prealcoholic would be regarded as someone who suffered from intensified dependency longings, but who outwardly tried to suppress any sign of his inner feelings. This interpretation is, of course, merely speculative, for we do not possess accurate information on the "real" feelings of the prealcoholic in childhood. One can argue, however, that once the disorder had set in, the person's defenses collapsed and these latent traits were openly manifested.

Second, we know that alcoholics in childhood were subjected to experiences that should lead to intensified dependency needs and to confusion in their self-images. The previous chapters have shown that alcoholics were often raised in conflictful, antagonistic homes by emotionally erratic and unstable mothers. Their background seemed to lead to dependency conflict—an unsureness concerning the satisfaction of heightened dependency desires. One way to handle these heightened, yet culturally disapproved, desires would be to repress the dependent urges. This, in fact, appeared to be the solution preferred by the alcoholics in childhood—by aggression, by denying dependent relations, by asserting self-confidence, the alcoholics may have been saying, in effect, "I don't care whether I am loved. I am strong, independent, every inch a man. We men don't need maternal care."

Third, other influences in childhood—paternal antagonism and escapism, for example—also might lead to this overemphasis on independence and masculinity. Deprived of a stable model to emulate, such children would grasp at any example that would assure them of a sense of identity. In the foregoing chapters we have seen that the prealcoholic was deprived of a clear perception of the male role. In stressing his aggressive masculinity, the prealcoholic child may have accepted the most readily available self-image—the example of aggressive manhood which is constantly and attractively offered through the mass media and other culturally acceptable examples. By asserting his "manhood," this type of person could overcome, at least temporarily, his basic confusion.

Thus, it is possible to speculate that the potentially alcoholic personality develops in this fashion:

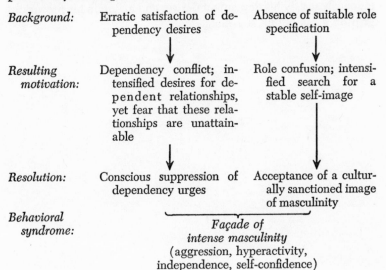

Background:	Erratic satisfaction of dependency desires	Absence of suitable role specification
Resulting motivation:	Dependency conflict; intensified desires for dependent relationships, yet fear that these relationships are unattainable	Role confusion; intensified search for a stable self-image
Resolution:	Conscious suppression of dependency urges	Acceptance of a culturally sanctioned image of masculinity
Behavioral syndrome:	*Façade of intense masculinity* (aggression, hyperactivity, independence, self-confidence)	

To resolve his inner conflicts by assuming a "masculine façade" is inherently precarious. His dependency needs continue to plague him, yet his role as an aggressive, independent male precludes their satisfaction. As he reaches adulthood, even further suppression of dependent urges is demanded of him by society; he must become a breadwinner, the leader of his family, a pillar of his community. In other words, his cultural role requires that he satisfy the dependent needs of others; he must, according to society's restrictions, largely deny dependent satisfactions to himself. Thus, if he tries to live up to this role (and, even more difficult, to maintain his intensified image of masculinity), he dooms himself to continual repression. If he chooses, on the other hand, to strive for open satisfaction of his heightened dependency desires, the price is high: he must relinquish not only his cultural role, but also his masculine self-image—his sense of identity and significance—which has been built up only through intense repression.

At some point in adulthood, this type of person learns that alcohol may provide a compromise solution to his conscious or unconscious dilemma. Through heavy drinking, generally regarded as masculine behavior, he may come to think that he can simultaneously satisfy his dependent desires and maintain his precarious grip on a masculine self-image.

9

CONCLUSIONS: THE NATURE OF ALCOHOLISM

In this book, we have attempted to unravel the origins of alcoholism, one of America's more serious social problems. The significance of this research, its justification, lies in certain unique methodological characteristics.

First, and most important, the research is longitudinal in nature. It is based on a sample of 255 urban, relatively lower-class boys who were participants in the Cambridge-Somerville Youth Project. Originally selected and observed in the 1930's, these boys were then traced to adulthood. A minority of the subjects became alcoholics, the great majority did not. By statistically comparing these two groups, we have distinguished certain physiological, personality, and familial traits that set the alcoholics apart as a distinctive human type *before* the onset of their disorder. It has thus been possible to eliminate some of the retrospective biases and confusions that have plagued previous analyses of the problem.

Second, our definition of alcoholism, while not all-encompassing, is open to replication by other scientists. An operational definition of alcoholism in terms of community standards (arrests for drunkenness, contact with social agencies, clinics, mental hospitals, or Alcoholics Anonymous) allows other scientists to compare different samples and check the validity of our generalizations as they apply to other groups. (Perhaps it should be noted again that we do not know the extent to which these findings pertain to people who are defined as alcoholic in different ways or to those who succumb to addiction in middle age; it may be, for example, that samples composed of private, middle-aged, psychoanalytic, or sanitarium patients would differ significantly from our alcoholic subjects.)

Third, the original selection of the sample furnished both a fair number of adult alcoholics and a large number of nondeviants. In the 1930's, half of the boys were selected for study because they were regarded as "maladjusted" children (primarily as potentially delinquent children). They eventually provided a sizable group of adult alcoholics. The others in the sample were chosen for their "normality," thus insuring sufficient nondeviant subjects for statistical comparisons. Equipped with a substantial control group of "normal" people, we were therefore able to avoid the errors that may appear in analyzing a small number of atypical individuals.

Fourth, since 255 boys were closely observed over a five-year period of their childhood by many different people, a number of possibly contaminating factors were probably eliminated. Direct observation by the counselors (and verbatim reports of these observations) meant that the subjects and their families were seen in a variety of situations and that many facets of their behavior (not just self-reports, or answers to questionnaires or tests, or responses in a particular experiment) could be used as the basis of analysis. The fact that these observations were carried on over a period of years meant that the analysis would be based on an extensive cross section of their daily lives, not only on their behavior in extraordinary situations. Because many different people (an average of four counselors and four other staff members) made these observations, the errors that may result from the biases of a single observer were counteracted by reports from other observers.

Fifth, since the original observers did not know that their material would eventually be used to analyze alcoholism, and the raters who later categorized the subjects' backgrounds did not know which boys had become alcoholics, the possibility that preconceived theories about the causes of alcoholism blinded the staff with certain prejudices was eliminated. Before rating the subjects, each type of behavior or trait to be identified was clearly defined. The interrater reliability, as the appendix shows, was high.

We have some faith, therefore, in the validity and eventual usefulness of the reseach. To achieve a balanced picture concerning the significance of the study, however, one must be aware of the deficiencies of our approach. Because the original observations were made by a heterogeneous group of people, some possibly relevant factors have been omitted owing to a lack of information or a lack of reliability. Biases of the original observations (overlooking some incidents, emphasizing others) may obscure some potentially important results. The unique characteristics of the sample may render some of the conclusions atypical. The small number of cases makes one necessarily hesitate to make generalizations about *all* alcoholics. A lack of subtlety in some of the measures (e.g., the metabolic examinations); a failure to use certain methods for tapping unconscious motivations; the lack of information on the adult lives of the subjects—these and many other gaps in the research could be specified by the perceptive critic.

Although we recognize these deficiencies, we do not believe that the research has been paralyzed by them. We would argue, rather, that the methodological virtues of the research tend to outweigh the methodological faults. The correctness of this opinion, as of all social scientific views about the disorder, will eventually be tested by additional longitudinal studies aimed at the prediction of alcoholism. If the causal pattern which is summarized in the next pages proves its predictive power, and therefore contributes to the prevention of alcoholism, then this book will be justified.

THE USE OF THE CONCEPT OF CAUSATION IN THIS STUDY

Throughout the book, we have made implicit causal generalizations; the reader who is acquainted with the philosophy of science may well question the justification of these conclusions. Therefore, we believe that it is important to make explicit our assumptions concerning the concept of causation in human behavior.

The concept of causation tends to be avoided by contemporary social scientists. Terms such as "relationship," "correlation," or "significant connection" are often substituted for the more explicit word, "cause." This reluctance is understandable. Philosophically, social scientists are well aware of Hume's definitive attack on the perception of causal connections. Perhaps, too, they are loath to confess to "the felt necessity of mind" which Hume believed composed the causal inference. Historically, social scientists remember too well those early theorists who thought they had discovered certain definitive causes of human actions—only to be thoroughly disproved by the course of history or by scientific evidence.

Two additional factors seem to us to be responsible for a general reluctance on the part of social scientists to make causal inferences. First, with natural science as a model, we recognize our deficiencies in predicting events of human behavior. Second, as a group, we hesitate to suggest that human beings do not have some leverage for "free choice"—by which we mean an internal strength or moral power to overcome whatever inherited or environmental influences might otherwise lead to socially obnoxious behavior.

In the natural sciences, until the advent of Heisenberg's principle, which (to some extent) undermined the classical concept of causation itself, a single failure in prediction was considered reason to question the completeness of a causal explanation. Social scientists, in contrast, have only rarely been able to predict behavior with perfect accuracy. In fact, many of the best predictive devices in the social sciences (e.g., some intelligence test scores) are acknowledged not to be themselves causally related to the events which they predict.

Nevertheless, we would like to point to conditions which, we believe, allow the justifiable use of the "causative" concept within social science, despite the failure in perfect prediction of behavior.

In our opinion when a valid assertion of causation is made, that is, when event A is correctly described as the sufficient and complete (necessary) cause of event B, essentially the statement can be reduced to the form: "Whenever event A occurs, event B will follow; and whenever event B has occurred, event A has preceded it." Evidence for the validity of such a statement lies in the correct prediction of events.

Although both forms of science accept this standard of validity for causal inferences, the matter under observation differs. The gross similarities among classes of material with which the physical scientist deals tend to outweigh the differences. Thus, in laboratory sciences most relevant variables can be held constant simultaneously; in other natural sciences, the theorist can generally accumulate a large enough number of cases with close enough resemblances to test his predictions readily and correct his theories if necessary.

In the social sciences, perhaps because the observer is a member of his species, a potential object of his own type of experiments, the differences often seem to outweigh the similarities. The difficulty of identifying members of a race with which we are unfamiliar illustrates how we emphasize the similarities among things different from ourselves. Each man considers himself unique and therefore has a tendency to see differences among men. (This suggests that from the point of view of, say, an atom, it might be extremely difficult to perceive the similarities among atoms.) Yet the discovery of general laws and of specific causes of behavior in any form of matter fundamentally depends upon the existence and perception of similarities.

Furthermore, one cannot easily conduct laboratory experiments to test theories of causation regarding the more complex behavior syndromes. Even assuming one knows the relevant conditions (e.g., the mother's attitude toward the child, in psychology, or the amount of mass discontent, in history) one cannot artificially hold these constant.

Although the delineation of a group varies according to the perspective of the observer and the nature of the analysis, it might be important to note that the physical scientist does not attempt to predict the behavior of particular, individual units (e.g., *this* molecule, *this* atom, or *this* electron). Thus, while a chemist predicts that when hydrogen and oxygen are mixed, under specified conditions they will unite, he does not attempt to indicate which molecule of hydrogen will unite with which atom of oxygen. Or in describing the composition of molecules by indicating the number of electrons in the outer ring, he makes no prediction regarding which electron will provide the bond between atoms. Thus, even the natural sciences give little support to the proposition that every event has a sufficient and complete cause.

It has commonly been assumed that either a particular event is caused or it is not caused. We propose, on the other hand, that causation be considered as a continuum—one kind of event may be more (or less) caused than another kind of event. One need not assume that predictive failures are due exclusively to errors or ignorance of the observer, or that corrections or improvements in prediction are impossible. Perhaps at the level of the "unique" (defined as "a fundamental unit within any operation"), causative explanations can only, even theoretically, be given in terms of probabilities which approach, but never attain, 100 per cent. Thus, a *cause* of a particular event would be best considered as a *condition that limits possibilities*. If any event is completely predictable (i.e., an event for which a sufficient and complete cause is theoretically discoverable), its possibilities have been limited to one, and may be said to be completely determined.

Possibilities (like "groups") depend on the observer's perspective and his analytical scope. Thus, a thin coin about to be tossed may be said to have two possibilities: "heads" or "tails." If one side is weighted, these possibilities become limited to one and the weight is considered to be the cause of its landing in the position it does. The coin, however, may be said to have three possibilities: "heads," "tails," and "on end"; from this perspective, the shape is a limiting condition (cause), preventing the coin from landing on end.

One must bear in mind, when considering the differences between natural and social science, the extensive history of natural science and the relative youth of social science. The natural sciences have long emphasized causal explanations. The social sciences have placed considerable emphasis upon "indicators,"* which need not be causally related to the events they predict. Because of the greater need for predicting human behavior, or because of the greater difficulty in analyzing its causes, social scientists have been attempting to find reliable "litmus papers" for various types of events (e.g., economic indices to predict depres-

---

* The term "indicator" will be used to mean "an event not causally related to a second event which it can be used to predict with varying degrees of accuracy.

sions, intelligence tests to predict school performance). In its early stages, natural science accepted as complete causal explanations what later appeared as only partial causes. Nevertheless, many of these early causal explanations seem to have been essential steps to the more complete explanations that followed.

These differences between natural and social sciences—especially those pertaining to the nature of the material being studied—suggest that a fundamental philosophical mistake is involved in the reluctance of social scientists to take hold of the causal concept.

If this analysis of the concept of "cause" is correct (it should be remembered that when possibilities have been reduced to one, the event is completely predictable), the social scientist who discovers what truly limits possibilities of behavior justifiably designates it as being "casually related" to the behavior that follows.

This approach to causation leaves unanswered the question: To what extent is all human behavior caused (i.e., constrained, determined) by prior events? In some areas, where there is extremely accurate predictability—e.g., the effects of specific forms of brain damage—one is inclined to say that the resulting forms of behavior are totally determined. We believe that neither morality nor science is served by assuming that particular areas of behavior are not similarly determined. If prior events do limit the possibilities of a person's behavior, and if some forms of behavior are considered undesirable (e.g., murder, alcoholism), then surely it is more effective to attempt to alter the limiting conditions than to appeal to "free will" in vain.

To recapitulate: The sufficient and *complete cause* (or the sufficient and necessary cause) of an event B would be the series of events A that bears such a relationship to B that whenever A occurs B follows and whenever B occurs A has preceded it. A *partial cause* of an event B' is the series of events A' that increases the probability that event B' will occur. The partial cause approaches a complete cause in direct ratio to the increase in probability that event B' will follow if and only if events A' have occurred. One need not decide *a priori* whether any particular event has a complete cause, that is, whether that type of event is at least theoretically completely predictable.

One further point needs to be made. As we have suggested,

"indicators" as well as causes enable accurate predictions. How do they differ? How can they be distinguished?

Of course, an indicator can never give more accurate predictions than can a cause (there must be limitations on possibilities before any external signs can be used to predict a consequent event "significantly better than chance"). An indicator is related only unilaterally to what it indicates. Thus, the perfect indicator would be so related to an event that whenever the indication occurred, the event would occur; but it would not be true that whenever the event occurred, the indication had occurred.

Before concluding that the causes of alcoholism have been ascertained, we must await proof that alcoholism occurs if—and *only* if—events A have preceded it. For the moment, we must base our analysis on the fact that certain "A events" have occurred significantly more frequently in the backgrounds of alcoholics than of nonalcoholics. Because, at least in our sample, we have found some evidence that alcoholism occurs only in the presence of at least one of those conditions we have designated as "causes" and because these findings lead to what we believe is a consistent theory, we have inferred that at least some of the *causes* of alcoholism have been discovered. Further research, we hope, will clarify these relationships.

SUMMARY OF THE CAUSES OF ALCOHOLISM

In the preceding chapters we have pointed to numerous conditions that appear to compose the causes of alcoholism. In attempting to make a coherent theory out of the many significant relationships we have found, we have centered on three types of external pressures: family background, cultural pressure, and the adult situation. The interaction of these environmental pressures with personality structure can perhaps best be summarized in the model on page 151.

Three qualifications to this model must be stated. First, it may well be that future research will uncover a set of variables even more directly relevant to alcoholism. An investigation of the very first years of life, for example, might demonstrate that various experiences are of critical importance; or, perhaps, more subtle metabolic tests might reveal some type of biochemical deficiency

MODEL OF ALCOHOLISM

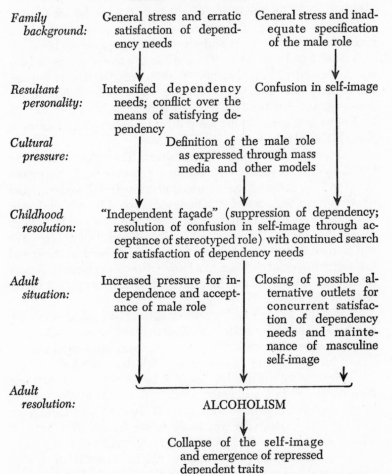

Family background: General stress and erratic satisfaction of dependency needs | General stress and inadequate specification of the male role

Resultant personality: Intensified dependency needs; conflict over the means of satisfying dependency | Confusion in self-image

Cultural pressure: Definition of the male role as expressed through mass media and other models

Childhood resolution: "Independent façade" (suppression of dependency; resolution of confusion in self-image through acceptance of stereotyped role) with continued search for satisfaction of dependency needs

Adult situation: Increased pressure for independence and acceptance of male role | Closing of possible alternative outlets for concurrent satisfaction of dependency needs and maintenance of masculine self-image

Adult resolution: ALCOHOLISM

Collapse of the self-image and emergence of repressed dependent traits

that is related to the causation of addiction. We cannot maintain, therefore, that the model exhausts the theoretical possibilities. Second, it is clear that the factors summarized in the following pages are not necessarily independent. Certain negative factors "go together"—ambivalent mothers, for example, were often deviant in behavior, were often married to rejecting husbands, and were often involved in intense familial conflicts. To treat these factors as independent "causes" of alcoholism is, to some extent, arbitrary. Third, some of the elements in this model are frankly speculative—we lack information on the unconscious needs of the prealcoholic in childhood and we lack information on his adult experiences and responses. Thus, while the model seems to be a reasonable extrapolation of our empirical results, it goes beyond the material and attempts to explain why certain childhood experiences are statistically associated with adult behavior.

Let us now examine the reasons for including these factors in the theoretical scheme:

1. *Family background: General stress:* The potential alcoholic had undergone a variety of frustrating experiences: he was more likely to have suffered from various neurological disorders; more likely to have been raised in a family disrupted by a high degree of conflict and basic disagreement; and more likely to have been reared in a family characterized by incest and illegitimacy. We can assume that these influences create a high level of stress and insecurity in a child and lead to a basic unsureness about his proper role in life. This stress can be expressed in many ways, not necessarily in alcoholism.

2. *Family background: Erratic satisfaction of dependency needs:* The major force which seemed to lead a person under high stress to express his anxiety in alcoholism was the erratic frustration of his dependency desires. The prealcoholic often came from an environment in which his desire to be loved was satisfied and then frustrated in a strikingly erratic fashion. Typically, he had been raised by a mother who alternated between loving indulgence and overt rejection, who was likely to see herself as a "martyr" whose own interests she had begrudgingly sacrificed to the interests of her family, who also tended to react to crises in an escapist manner and to participate in various kinds of deviant behavior. An intense degree of parental antagonism also distinguished the alcoholic's family from the nondeviant's. In addition, the potential alcoholic's father tended to regard the boy's mother with low esteem.

3. *Resultant personality: Conflict over heightened dependency desires:* We reasoned that these influences had two major effects: (1) boys raised in such environments underwent an intensification of their need for love; and (2) they felt great anxiety about the

satisfaction of this heightened need. We are unable to present direct empirical evidence for these two deductions. From a variety of experimental studies, nevertheless, comes evidence that erratic satisfaction of any drive leads to an intensification of the need. Moreover, it seems reasonable to assume that conflict would be generated whenever a person is alternately rewarded and then punished for the same kind of behavior. The prealcoholic was raised, on the one hand, by a mother who sometimes indulged him, who talked constantly of her sacrifices, who titillated him with various examples of sexual deviance. On the other hand, the same mother would, at times, berate the child and fail to come to his aid in critical situations. In the background, the boy's father talked disparagingly of the mother's failings. This strange combination of rewarding and punishing the child's need for love and maternal care would, it seems reasonable to suppose, cause extreme dependency conflict in the child.

4. *Family background: Inadequate specification of the male role:* The potential alcoholic was not offered a clear, specific image of manhood. His father tended to be antagonistic and tried to escape from the pressures of critical situations. The prealcoholic's parents did not enforce high demands that he accept responsibility. In short, such children were raised in environments in which the responsibilities of the male role were neither exemplified nor enforced.

5. *Resultant personality: Confusion in self-image:* One major result of these experiences was confusion in the child's self-image. The typical alcoholic lacked specific definitions of the male role. He was commonly exposed to highly erratic experiences—at times, his parents might approve a certain action; at other times, they might ignore or actually punish him for the same thing. In many ways, his father's behavior contradicted the usual stereotype of the male's role in American society. Radio, the newspapers, his teachers, the movies, all picture the typical male as being responsible, courageous, law-abiding, and loving. The alcoholic's parents, particularly his father, tended to be the opposite: cowardly, rejecting, and often deviant. It seems likely, therefore, that the child raised under the influence of such contradictory examples would be confused over his role in life.

6. *Childhood resolution: Creation of an independent façade:*

The person who has been subjected to these experiences often seeks to resolve his various conflicts behind a façade that can satisfy his dependency conflict, end his confusion about his self-image, and ensure the approval of his society. The evidence has indicated that the typical prealcoholic creates an independent, super-masculine façade. He tends to be aggressive, outwardly self-confident, highly independent. In other words, the potential alcoholic accepts the American stereotype of masculinity and then plays this role to the hilt. We would assume that his choice of an independent self-image involved the suppression of dependency desires. Thus, by becoming a highly independent male, he achieves a temporary resolution of his disturbing conflicts.

Underneath his façade of self-reliant manhood, the typical alcoholic, we have proposed, continues to feel anxious, to suffer conflict, and to be desirous of dependent relationships. If one assumes that his traumatic early experiences produce a permanently heightened desire for dependency, then it follows that his conscious attempt at suppressing these desires is doomed to failure. Outwardly, he might attempt to maintain a façade of independence; inwardly, he would long for supporting, maternal care. Consequently, he would attempt to satisfy these forbidden urges in various vicarious ways; simultaneously he would strive to protect and defend his self-image and to assure vicarious satisfaction of his repressed dependent needs. This search for vicarious satisfaction might take him down a number of different channels; he might try to find a wife who would serve as a pseudo-mother, he might join social organizations that would offer him a sense of belonging and of camaraderie, or he might choose an occupation where he could be under the care of comforting figures.

7. *Adult situation: Closing possible alternative outlets for expression of dependency:* As an adult, the typical prealcoholic would involve himself in a quixotic quest to satisfy his dual desires to be independent and dependent. Because of his background, certain outlets would be closed to him. As we have shown in the previous chapters, the alcoholic was raised by parents who were nominally religious, but not deeply committed to their faith. Raised in such an environment, it is likely that the prealcoholic, too, would not put much reliance on the church. Thus, one major outlet for his conflicts—submergence in a strong religious faith—

would be denied him. Unlike the strongly religious person, the prealcoholic would tend to withdraw from the comforts of a church; he could not express his dependent longings by seeking direction from God, the priest, the minister, or the elders. He could not find, in the church, the sure direction and guidance that he lacked in his early life.

In addition to the religious channel, other outlets are denied the typical middle-class male (among whom we found a significantly higher proportion of alcoholics). Such possible outlets as professional prizefighting (with the manager taking over the "maternal" role) or soldiering as careers are largely taboo for the middle class. Unless he wrenched himself from his entire ideological background, the prealcoholic would thus be denied certain satisfactions available to lower-class males. Simultaneously, the middle-class values of achievement and success would press the prealcoholic toward accepting the role of independent masculinity.

8. *The function of alcoholism:* Alcohol would be a major outlet available to such a person. When intoxicated, he could achieve feelings of warmth, comfort, and omnipotence. His strong desires to be dependent would be satisfied. At the same time, he could maintain his image of independence and self-reliance. The hard drinker in American society is pictured as tough, extroverted, and manly—exactly the masculine virtues the alcoholic strives to incorporate into his own self-image.

With his basic psychological make-up, together with the social pressures, the absence of alternative resolutions, and the lack of strong proscriptions against imbibing, such a person would be likely to succumb to alcohol.

9. *Collapse of the self-image:* The reports on the lives of adult alcoholics indicate that the severe effects of alcoholism do not become manifest until middle age. Typically, the alcoholic begins drinking only at parties, then on week-end binges, then every day. He moves from drinking only at night to drinking in the evening, then to drinking at lunch and in the morning. He finds that he is "blacking-out" after sessions of heavy drinking, that he must sneak drinks at parties. Finally, his life becomes oriented around securing his daily supply of alcohol.

We believe that the confirmed alcoholic increases his intake of alcohol because intoxication satisfies his dependency urges and obliterates reminders of his own inadequacies. We assume that his character is organized around a quest for dependency; in alcohol he finds a permanent, easily available, and, at first, non-threatening method of satisfaction.

The alcoholic's almost continuous state of intoxication naturally interferes with many other aspects of his life. His occupational efficiency falters, he loses his role as the "rock" of the family, his image of himself as an independent male is undermined in various ways. The evidence indicates that he is usually a social outcast and that he finds himself in profound conflict with his wife and family.

Research also indicates that unless the alcoholic finds some resolution of his conflicts (e.g., by membership in Alcoholics Anonymous), his repressed traits of dependency, inferiority, and passivity become openly manifested; his attempt to maintain a façade of independent manliness collapses.

SOME SPECULATIONS ON THE ROLE OF ADULT EXPERIENCES
IN CAUSATION

We have been almost solely concerned with those early experiences that apparently produced alcoholism. We have also speculated on the adult lives of alcoholics. We have argued, for example, that the alcoholic's dependent desires continue in adulthood, that his character becomes dominated by his needs. We have offered only indirect evidence for this view: we know that in childhood the prealcoholic underwent a series of experiences productive of dependency conflict; that adult alcoholics often exhibited dependent and passive traits *after* the disorder had manifested itself. Thus, we had evidence that indicated dependency conflict both before and after the person became alcoholic. Direct evidence about the intervening adult years is, however, lacking.

In a general sense, we know that the prealcoholics—simply because they were adult males in America—were subjected to a number of pressures. Our culture expects boys to become increasingly independent, self-reliant, and masculine as they approach manhood. The prealcoholics, like all American men, were pressed by their culture to renounce their dependent desires even more

strongly than before. Such demands—imposed on an already unstable character structure—undoubtedly created great anxiety in
the prealcoholics. Thus, in contemporary America the cultural definition of the male role is an important intervening variable in our
analysis of the causes of alcoholism. In societies where "masculinity" is defined with less stringency (or where acceptable outlets
for dependency desires are provided), the pattern of the potential
alcoholic's life might be fundamentally different.

Even in contemporary America there are many relatively acceptable outlets for the person caught in dependency conflict.
What events in adulthood would lead him toward the deviant path
of alcoholism? What adult events serve to trigger his disorder, to
push him beyond incipient alcoholism to the point of outright
addiction? Unfortunately, there is little objective information on
this problem. One way of answering the question is by reviewing
the many case histories, biographies, and autobiographies of alcoholics. These sources (necessarily retrospective in nature) report
only those events which the alcoholics themselves, or their biogra-
phers, viewed as precipitating factors. Some sources indicate that
alcoholics have typically undergone three adult experiences which
seem to tip the balance in favor of alcoholism. First, they are
exposed to specific environments in which hard drinking is presented as an attractive "style of life." This usually occurs either in
late adolescence or early manhood. Second, they are subjected
to a series of experiences which severely frustrate their desires to
be dependent; they "try out" alternative ways of securing dependent satisfactions, only to meet with frustration. Third, various
events seriously undermine their self-image of masculine independence.

Let us examine each of these adult "triggering" incidents more
closely.

1. *Drinking as an attractive way of life:* In our society adver-
tisements and the mass media present the imbibing of alcohol as
a thoroughly enjoyable process. Moreover, alcohol is readily available, even among "dry" communities. The availability and attractiveness of alcohol in modern America are important factors in
our generally high rate of alcoholism. America contains few her-
oin, marijuana, or peyote addicts—primarily because society so

strongly disapproves of such addiction and makes it extremely difficult for a person to secure these drugs. In certain Indian cultures, drugs can be secured as easily as we can get alcohol. Whereas drugs possibly serve the same purpose and appeal to the same type of character structure as does alcohol, their relative scarcity would lead to a low rate of drug addiction, while alcohol's abundance would contribute to a concentration on it.

Beyond his general exposure to an American environment which encourages drinking, the alcoholic has typically been subjected to experiences in adulthood that may give him further encouragement to drink heavily.

"Mr. G," a case described by Ruth Fox, illustrates this point.[1] Mr. G was an advertising executive who, as part of his job, toured the country with a radio program; it was on this tour that his addiction began:

> Wherever he went he found that his job involved a lot of drinking: he had been told he should entertain the local station bigwigs and was given a liberal expense account to do so, but the local station bigwigs had their own liberal expense accounts with which to entertain him. In one city after another, one night after another, G tried hard to drink, drink for drink, with men to whom hard drinking came easy. It was a matter of pride with G, and at the same time he imagined that it was a matter of good business. When the glasses began to empty, he felt that it was his responsibility to refill them—and he hoped always that the word would get back to New York that he, G, was a good fellow, a good two-fisted drinker, a sharp man in a business deal, but you could never get him drunk, he always had the agency's best interests at heart.[2]

After returning to New York, G found that his department head was an incipient alcoholic who insisted that G accompany him on morning drinking bouts in saloons near their office. G began to take up early morning drinking as a way to overcome his hangovers and he found that "blackouts" obscured his memory of drinking. As his life progressed, G became a confirmed alcoholic.

Such examples could readily be multiplied. They add up to the conclusion that the typical alcoholic often *remembers* having undergone experiences in which alcohol led to a more glorious way of life. We emphasize the "remembrance" of these events, for they can be interpreted in several ways. One might assume that the typical alcoholic has actually lived in an environment which objectively encouraged hard drinking; the environment could thus be regarded as a partially causative, precipitating factor in the disorder. It could be alternatively argued, however, that the potential alcoholic *seeks out* the situations—cocktail parties, friendships, certain occupations—in which drinking is encouraged; the environments themselves may not be causally important. It is difficult to decide between these two explanations; it seems probable, however, that adult drinking experiences play some type of "triggering" role in alcoholism. To take an extreme example, a potential alcoholic who was exposed *only* to a Mennonite community—one which strongly disapproved of any kind of drinking—would be highly unlikely to become addicted. On the other hand, if a potential alcoholic's adult environment offers alcohol as an enjoyable, acceptable outlet, his chances of succumbing to addiction would be considerably increased.

2. *Frustration of dependency urges in adulthood:* As we have pointed out, the potential alcoholic, simply by being a man in modern America, must sacrifice many of his dependency longings; he must strive to be self-reliant, brave, independent, and resourceful. As an adult, he is exposed to continuing frustration of his heightened dependency longings. Beyond this, however, it appears that he often suffers from certain specific and frustrating incidents.

The break-up of a previously satisfying marriage is one such event. Harold Maine, for example, after battling his alcoholic tendencies, returned to his wife, fully expecting a loving welcome. Instead, he discovered that she expected him to fall back into his old drinking habits. A final battle with her resulted in the end of the marriage:

I went home to an empty house that evening. Now jealousy, an impotent rage, and loneliness quarreled within me. I discovered some new things about myself. After all my lonely years as a vagrant, cook, and dubious troubadour, when I had been almost all things to myself, marriage had made me a different kind of man. I'd gotten used to living in the eyes and heart of someone close to me, of acting to please her, of restraining myself in order not to displease her. In this transformation I had become almost nothing to myself; I now seemed incapable of doing things for myself alone. Maybe something that I had been denied in my childhood had cropped up and was having its season. . . . I needed a guiding force.[3]

Clearly, in his marriage, Maine had found a rewarding way of expressing his longings to be dependent. His wife had served as a "guiding force," a comforting, loving, maternal figure. Unfortunately, this pattern collapsed. Almost immediately, Maine turned back to alcohol.

Everyone is subject to some frustrations of dependency desires either by a disappointing marriage, by an anxiety-provoking occupation, by the collapse of previously satisfying social contacts, or by more minor experiences. The normal person can go through these frustrations without permanent scars. For the potential alcoholic, however, such incidents could have profound meaning: they indicate to him that adulthood, like childhood, is fraught with frustration of his dependent longings. Undoubtedly, many potential alcoholics resolve their conflicts without turning to liquor. If they can find a mate who will totally satisfy them or an occupation, an avocation, or a social institution that will fulfill their dependent needs, they can be saved from addiction. If, however, they continue to meet frustration of their dependent desires in adulthood, they will often turn to alcohol as a way of alleviating their inner conflict.

3. *Attacks on the independent self-image:* It has already been demonstrated that prealcoholics tend to be aggressive, manly, and independent. Events that undermine this masculine self-image and expose the deficiencies in the façade should heighten the tendency to seek comfort in alcohol. Such experiences are, indeed, commonly found in the adult lives of alcoholics.

Harold Maine's ill-fated marriage was one such situation. Virginia, his wife, put extraordinary demands on his abilities; in his career as a writer, she expected him to achieve the heights. Constant pressure from her only put Maine into greater conflict: "She accepted me as a genius and would have no less. . . . When I found myself unable to escape her by distance and indifference, I would then escape through drink. This at first and for a long time she took to be a portion of my genius. Being called a genius made me uncomfortable; I knew what I was."[4]

Constantly exposed to a close scrutiny by his ambitious wife, Maine was forced to recognize that his self-image did not correspond with reality; to admit this incongruence was impossible for

him, so he sought comfort in drink. A later series of incidents in
Maine's life brought about a recurrence of alcoholism. After a
period of relative sobriety, Maine wrote a novel and sent it eagerly
to a publisher. It was flatly rejected:

My failure was held up for all to see. I cringed like an exposed
embezzler. The novel made the publishers uncomfortable, or so several
said, but their discomfort must have been mild compared to mine. Since
I was living on Jean's income [his second wife] this failure made me
feel that people were critical of me.[5]

Once again, his image of himself was deflated—this time, by
an objective failure which "everyone" witnessed. Maine decided
that he should change his occupation, that he should become a
self-reliant businessman. The criticism caused by rejection of his
novel made him remember his stepfather's advice:

It threw me back into my old relationship with my stepfather. Hard
work, industry, and finally a business are the ways a man makes his
mark in the world, so he had preached. I listened to his sermon and
sought his approval. . . .
There was a small business for sale that I could take care of and
finance. It required a great deal of hard work and much hardheaded-
ness, something of which I am devoid. Because of the failure of my
novel and my insecurity about our life, Jean was enthusiastic.[6]

Maine bought the business and threw himself into the work
with enthusiasm. But, in time, the business failed. Faced with
another rebuff to his self-image—an attack that pointed up once
again his essential dependence on others—Maine turned back to
liquor. This time, he landed on Skid Row.

Because their hold on a self-image is so precarious, people like
Maine react intensely to defeats. Unlike the more "normal" person,
who may go through life without being aware that reality is clash-
ing with his self-image, the potential alcoholic is constantly on
the alert. If he meets with a frustrating situation, this may well
prove to be the trigger of addiction.

If someone who is characterized by a potentially alcoholic personality syndrome passes through all three of these stages, his
destiny as an alcoholic would seem to be assured. If, in contrast,
he lived in a society where alcohol was highly disapproved or
where he could find institutionalized opportunities to satisfy his

dependency longings and protect his precarious self-image, the chances of addiction would be lessened, if not eliminated entirely.

SOME SPECULATIONS ON FEMALE ALCOHOLISM

In modern America, alcoholism is primarily a male disorder. Approximately five times as many men as women succumb to addiction. Although we lack any definitive evidence on alcoholism in women, we can speculate indirectly on the reasons for the relatively lower rate of female alcoholism.

Undoubtedly, a certain proportion of women in modern America exhibit a character closely resembling that of the male alcoholic—accompanied by a heightened level of stress, intensified dependency longings, and confusion over their role in life. In this sense, then, they could be considered as "potential" alcoholics. The adult female role in American society, however, gives little encouragement to drinking and allows the expression of these traits without resort to alcohol addiction:

1. Adult women in our society are not *supposed* to be hard drinkers; men are allowed, even encouraged, to drink heavily at cocktail parties, fraternity gatherings, and other social occasions. A drunk woman faces sharp social disapproval. Such cultural control over women's drinking decreases the lures of liquor. In part, at least, changes in cultural attitudes toward female drinking could account for the rising rates of alcoholism among women.

2. American women are encouraged to be passively dependent. "The woman's place is in the home," under the care (or domination) of a protective male. A woman who suffers from intensified dependent longings can find satisfactions simply by living the role most approved by her society. Her conflicts can be assuaged through marriage and homemaking; her need for alcohol as a vicarious outlet is consequently reduced. Males, on the other hand, cannot assume a dependent position without encountering opposition from their society.

3. The possibility that woman's self-image will be seriously threatened by adult experiences is not as great. The woman's role is less demanding, more restricted. Thus, she may fail to perform her maternal-wifely role in a satisfactory way, but the chances that this failure will be exposed to the view of outsiders is rela-

tively slight. A man, on the other hand, can fail not only in his familial but also in his occupational role; the possibility that a man's self-image will be *publicly* deflated is greater.

Thus, the female role in American society—with its restrictions on drinking, its built-in channels for the expression of dependency, and its relatively lower level of frustration—militates against alcoholism. We believe, moreover, that some women who are most "feminine," who enjoy most intensely the dependent aspects of their role, are those who have undergone experiences that would lead to alcoholism in a man. (The situation is complicated, however, because some of these "feminine" women may have extremely consistent self-images.)

Whereas male alcoholism is "favored" by heightened dependency needs that conflict with expectations entailed in the masculine role, this conflict does not occur as frequently for the female in America. Perhaps as the woman's role becomes increasingly "masculine," the female potential alcoholic will find nonalcoholic satisfactions less available.

The female alcoholic is more likely to have a background of role confusion than one of dependency conflict. Her inability to accept her role could be the result of parental expectations that conflict with the cultural delineation of the female role, of an early environment that "punished" the girl's attempts to perform female role activities, or of a female model whose behavior is markedly different from "the norm." Again, because the cultural definition of the female role is in flux, we would expect increasing rates of alcoholism among women.

We have referred to the closing gap between male and female rates of addiction. In the nineteenth century, available evidence indicates that there were approximately twenty male alcoholics for every female alcoholic. Today, the ratio has substantially decreased. If our speculations are valid, the reasons for this historical change can be found in the changing definition of the female role in America. Compared to the nineteenth-century American society, twentieth-century American society disapproves of female drinking less stringently. In addition, occupational possibilities for women outside the home have vastly increased, while various technological changes have resulted in a decrease in the duties and attractiveness of homemaking. More than ever before, the female role has come to resemble the male role in society. Thus, while women's freedom has increased, the pressures have also increased; the chance that a woman can satisfy her needs through a wifely role have been progressively lessened. At the same time, the opportunities to use alcohol as an outlet have increased. The combination of these trends may account for the relative increase in female addiction.

Thus we come to the end of this monograph on alcoholism. Although our research leaves many unanswered questions, the findings suggest that the "predisposition" to alcoholism is established rather early in life, through the person's intimate experiences within his family. This theory is necessarily a speculative one, but it is supported not only by the new longitudinal data, but indirectly by such well-established facts as the male-female difference in rates of alcoholism.

Alcoholism, like crime, may be one of the unfortunate prices our society has to pay for the virtues of the "American way of life." Nevertheless, the uniquely pathological environments which specifically lead to the disorder may not be an inevitable part of our society. And if alcoholism is caused by early familial experiences, there is hope that our society may find the means to eliminate those influences that doom so many Americans to a life of alcoholic madness.

APPENDIX I

CATEGORIZATION OF THE SUBJECTS' BACKGROUNDS

The following is a copy of the rating sheets used for each of the boys and their families. Definitions of those categories which proved to be significantly related to alcoholism are included in the text.

(Name of boy)	(Group)	(Rater)

GENERAL FACTORS

1. Neighborhood: ——no information
   ——transitional ——residential

2. Race: ——no information
   a. ——white
   b. ——Negro
   c. ——mixed; father white
   d. ——mixed; mother white

3. Father's birthplace: ——no information
   ——U.S.A. ——outside U.S.A.

4. Cultural background: ——no information
   a. ——Italy
   b. ——Greece
   c. ——Portugal
   d. ——Ireland
   e. ——Western Europe
   f. ——Eastern Europe
   g. ——French Canada
   h. ——British Canada
   i. ——B.W.I.
   j. ——U.S.A.
   k. ——other

5. Ethnic allegiance of boy: ——no information
   a. ——accepts father's culture
   b. ——rejects father's culture
   c. ——inapplicable; no ethnic subculture

6. Community or subgroup solidarity: ——inadequate records
   ——present ——absent

FAMILY STRUCTURE

1. Parental unit: (mark more than one if applicable)
   a. ——natural parents living together
   b. ——mother unmarried
   c. ——parents separated; age of child: ——
   d. ——father committed suicide; age of child: ——

(family structure)

    e. ——father in prison; age of child: ——
    f. ——father in mental hospital; age of child: ——
    g. ——father deserted; age of child: ——
    h. ——father dead; age of child: ——
    i. ——mother in mental hospital; age of child: ——
    j. ——mother deserted; age of child: ——
    k. ——mother dead; age of child: ——

2. Significant adult other than parents:

    a. ——none noted
    b. ——supports parents
    c. ——independent of parents
    d. ——counter-influence

3. Number of children in family: ——

4. Age difference between boy and closest younger sibling (discount twins)
    ——years   ——no younger sibling

5. Age difference between boy and closest older sibling (discount twins)
    ——years   ——no older sibling

6. Family configuration:

    a. ——no brothers or sisters
    b. ——brothers; no sisters
    c. ——sisters; no brothers
    d. ——sisters and brothers

7. Boy's relative position in the family:

    a. ——only child
    b. ——only remaining child (another child died)
    c. ——only remaining child (another child living away from home)
    d. ——twin; no other children
    e. ——twin; oldest in family
    f. ——twin; middle
    g. ——twin; youngest
    h. ——oldest (no twin)
    i. ——middle (no twin)
    j. ——youngest (no twin)

Relation to siblings (mark most significant one)

8. Childhood: ——no information   9. Adolescence: ——no information

    a. ——no siblings at home   a. ——no siblings at home
    b. ——indifferent   b. ——indifferent
    c. ——companions   c. ——companions
    d. ——competitive   d. ——competitive
    e. ——antagonistic   e. ——antagonistic

10. Deviance within family:

    a. ——illegitimacy; probably threatening to boy
    b. ——illegitimacy; not threatening to boy

c. ———incest; probably threatening to boy
d. ———incest; not threatening to boy
e. ———neither illegitimacy nor incest

FAMILY INTERACTION

1. Parental dominance: ———no information
   a. ———father generally dominant
   b. ———mother generally dominant
   c. ———equal dominance
   d. ———only one parent at home

2. Father's esteem of mother: ———no indication
   ———moderate or high ———low

3. Mother's esteem of father: ———no indication
   ———moderate or high ———low

4. Parental role differentiation: ———no information
   a. ———highly, reversed
   b. ———highly, expected roles
   c. ———moderately differentiated
   d. ———no differentiation
   e. ———only one parent at home

5. Satisfaction with role activities of spouse: ———no indication
   a. ———both appear satisfied   c. ———mother dissatisfied
   b. ———father dissatisfied   d. ———both dissatisfied

6. Parental affection for each other: ———no indication
   a. ———natural parents; affectionate
   b. ———natural parents; sporadically affectionate
   c. ———natural parents; indifferent
   d. ———natural parents; antagonistic
   e. ———current parents affectionate
   f. ———current parents sporadically affectionate
   g. ———current parents indifferent
   h. ———current parents antagonistic

7. Parental conflict: ———no indication
   ———apparently none ———some ———considerable

8. Parental conflict about child: ———no indication
   ———apparently none ———some ———considerable

9. Parental conflict about values: ———no indication
   ———apparently none ———some

10. Parental conflict about alcohol: ———no indication
   ———apparently none ———some ———basic conflict in home

11. Parental conflict about money: ———no indication
   ———apparently none ———some ———basic conflict in home

12. Parental conflict about religion: ———no indication
   ———apparently none ———some ———basic conflict in home

(family interaction)

13. Parental comparison of boy to others: ——no indication
    a. ——few comparisons made
    b. ——generally favorable
    c. ——generally unfavorable
    d. ——variable

14. Boy's position in family: ——no indication
    a. ——"bright hope"
    b. ——pet or "mamma's boy"
    c. ——clown
    d. ——lone wolf
    e. ——"odd ball"
    f. ——trouble maker or "black sheep"
    g. ——no distinctive role

DISCIPLINE

1. Supervision during childhood: ——no information
   ——present   ——sporadic   ——absent

2. Expectations or demands: ——no information
   ——high   ——moderate   ——low

3. Major disciplinary area: ——no information
   a. ——generalized discipline
   b. ——aggression
   c. ——sex
   d. ——deception
   e. ——"bad companions"
   f. ——weakness
   g. ——achievement failure
   h. ——disrespect
   i. ——property upkeep
   j. ——personal cleanliness
   k. ——impulsiveness

Major disciplining agent of boy:

4. Childhood: ——no indication
   a. ——mother (or stepmother)
   b. ——father (or stepfather)
   c. ——older male sibling
   d. ——older female sibling
   e. ——other male
   f. ——other female

5. Adolescence: ——no indication
   a. ——mother (or stepmother)
   b. ——father (or stepfather)
   c. ——older male sibling
   d. ——older female sibling
   e. ——other male
   f. ——other female

6. Father's disciplinary technique: ——no information
   a. ——consistently punitive (include very harsh verbal abuse)
   b. ——erratically punitive
   c. ——consistent, nonpunitive
   d. ——inconsistent, nonpunitive
   e. ——extremely lax (almost no use of discipline)

7. Mother's disciplinary technique: ——no information
   a. ——consistently punitive (include very harsh verbal abuse)
   b. ——erratically punitive
   c. ——consistent, nonpunitive
   d. ——inconsistent, nonpunitive
   e. ——extremely lax (almost no use of discipline)

8. Use of threats: ——no indication
   ——extreme or frequent   ——little or none

9. Use of isolation: ———no indication
   ———frequent ———little or none

FATHER

1. Person rated (acting paternal figure at beginning of study)
   ———natural father ———stepfather ———other

2. Age of boy when father substitute entered family: ———

3. Religion: ———no information
   a. ———strong Catholic (every week)
   b. ———weak Catholic
   c. ———strong Protestant (every week)
   d. ———weak Protestant
   e. ———strong Jewish (every week or ritual adherence)
   f. ———weak Jewish
   g. ———agnostic or atheist

4. Occupation: ————————————(specify)
   a. ———professional   c. ———skilled tradesman
   b. ———white collar   d. ———unskilled worker

5. Employment: ———no information
   a. ———regularly employed
   b. ———irregularly employed
   c. ———unemployed (involuntarily)
   d. ———unemployed (voluntarily)

6. ———entrepreneurial ———bureaucratic ———varies or no indication

7. Age at birth of boy: ———

8. Education: ———no information
   a. ———no formal education
   b. ———attended grammar school; did not graduate (8th grade)
   c. ———graduated from grammar school; did not attend high school
   d. ———attended high school; did not graduate
   e. ———graduated from high school; no further schooling
   f. ———attended post–high school; did not graduate
   g. ———graduated from college
   h. ———graduated from other type of post–high school

9. Attitude toward boy: ———no indication
   a. ———actively affectionate
   b. ———passively affectionate
   c. ———marked alternation between affection and rejection
   d. ———actively rejecting
   e. ———passively rejecting

10. Mental condition: ———no indication
    ———psychotic ———neurotic ———neither

11. Stomach trouble: ———no health report on father
    ———yes ———none noted

(father)

12. Anxiety about health: ——no information
    ——realistic   ——unrealistic

13. Body care: ——no indication
    ——excessive   ——normal   ——inadequate (e.g., very sloppy)

14. Consumption of alcohol: ——no mention
    ——habitual or excessive   ——some   ——none

15. Situation for drinking: ——no information
    a. ——religious ritual only
    b. ——social traditional
    c. ——outside tradition (e.g., bars)

16. Attitude toward drinking: ——no information
    ——approves   ——neutral   ——disapproves (at least for others)

17. Ethnic maladjustment: ——no information
    ——yes   ——no   ——inapplicable

18. Social involvement: ——no information
    ——little participation   ——only informal   ——formal involvement

19. Attitude: ——no indication
    ——victim   ——neutral   ——self-confident

20. Role in family: ——no indication
    a. ——dictator
    b. ——leader
    c. ——passive
    d. ——stud

21. Feelings of grandiosity: ——no indication
    ——none   ——some   ——psychotic

22. Behavior (check all that are applicable):   ——no information
    a. ——alcoholic   d. ——irresponsible
    b. ——criminal   e. ——none of these
    c. ——sexually unfaithful

23. Masculinity: ——no indication
    a. ——highly masculine   c. ——dependent
    b. ——normally masculine   d. ——effeminate

24. Aggressiveness: ——no indication
    ——unrestrained   ——moderate   ——greatly inhibited

25. Reaction to crises: ——no indication
    a. ——withdraws   f. ——deserts
    b. ——becomes aggressive   g. ——remains indifferent
    c. ——drinks   h. ——seeks equilibrium (with-
    d. ——has sex relations   out facing problem)
    e. ——eats   i. ——faces realistically

26. Value emphasis: ——no indication
    a. ——enjoyment   d. ——achievement (including perfection)
    b. ——security   e. ——status ("success")
    c. ——popularity

27. Conscience orientation: ——no indication
    a. ——other-directed   e. ——other-directed, authoritarian
    b. ——authoritarian   f. ——other-directed, hedonist
    c. ——integral   g. ——integral, authoritarian
    d. ——hedonist

MOTHER

1. Person rated (acting maternal figure)
    ——natural mother   ——stepmother   ——other

2. Age of boy when mother substitute entered family: ——

3. Number of husbands mother has had: ——

4. Religion: ——no information
    a. ——strong Catholic (every week)
    b. ——weak Catholic
    c. ——strong Protestant (every week)
    d. ——weak Protestant
    e. ——strong Jewish (every week or ritual adherence)
    f. ——weak Jewish
    g. ——agnostic or atheist

5. Occuption (first 2 years of study):   ——no information
    a. ——housewife   d. ——factory worker
    b. ——clerical   e. ——servant
    c. ——saleswoman

6. Employment outside the home (first 2 yrs. of study):   ——no information
    ——regular   ——irregular   ——not employed outside home

7. Age at birth of boy: ——

8. Education: ——no information
    a. ——no formal education
    b. ——attended grammar school; did not graduate (8th grade)
    c. ——graduated from grammar school; did not attend high school
    d. ——attended high school; did not graduate
    e. ——graduated from high school; no further schooling
    f. ——attended post–high school; did not graduate
    g. ——graduated from college
    h. ——graduated from other type of post–high school

9. Attitude toward boy: ——no indication
    a. ——actively affectionate   d. ——actively rejecting
    b. ——passively affectionate   e. ——passively rejecting
    c. ——marked alternation between affection and rejection

10. Control of boy during childhood: ——no indication
    ——overly restrictive   ——normally   ——subnormally restrictive

11. Mental condition: ——no indication
    ——psychotic   ——neurotic   ——neither

12. Stomach trouble: ——no health report on mother
    ——yes   ——none noted

13. Anxiety about health: ——no information
    ——realistic   ——unrealistic

172   APPENDIX I

(mother)

14. Body care: ——no indication
    ——excessive   ——normal   ——inadequate (e.g., very sloppy)

15. Consumption of alcohol: ——no mention
    ——habitual or excessive   ——some   ——none

16. Situation for drinking: ——no information
    a. ——religious ritual only
    b. ——social traditional
    c. ——outside tradition (e.g., bars)

17. Attitude toward drinking: ——no information
    ——approves   ——neutral   ——disapproves (at least for others)

18. Ethnic maladjustment: ——no information
    ——yes   ——no   ——inapplicable

19. Social involvement: ——no information
    ——little participation   ——only informal   ——formal involvement

20. Attitude: ——no indication
    ——victim   ——neutral   ——self-confident

21. Role in family: ——no indication
    a. ——dictator   d. ——passive
    b. ——leader   e. ——neglecting
    c. ——"martyr"

22. Feelings of grandiosity: ——no indication
    ——none   ——some   ——psychotic

23. Behavior (check all that are applicable):   ——no information
    a. ——alcoholic   d. ——irresponsible
    b. ——criminal   e. ——none of these
    c. ——sexually unfaithful

24. Anxiety about sex: ——no indication
    ——apparently none   ——some   ——strong

25. Aggressiveness: ——no indication
    ——unrestrained   ——moderate   ——greatly inhibited

26. Encouragement of masculine activities (of boy):   ——no indication
    ——strongly encouraged   ——moderate or neutral   ——discouraged

27. Encouragement of independence: ——no indication
    ——strong   ——moderate or weak

28. Encouragement of dependency: ——no indication
    ——strong   ——moderate or weak

29. Reaction to crises: ——no indication
    a. ——withdraws   f. ——deserts
    b. ——becomes aggressive   g. ——remains indifferent
    c. ——drinks   h. ——seeks equilibrium (with-
    d. ——has sex relations   out facing problem)
    e. ——eats   i. faces realistically

30. Value emphasis: ——no indication
   a. ——enjoyment   d. ——achievement (including perfection)
   b. ——security   e. ——status ("success")
   c. ——popularity

31. Conscience orientation: ——no indication
   a. ——other-directed   e. ——other-directed authoritarian
   b. ——authoritarian   f. ——other-directed hedonist
   c. ——integral   g. ——integral authoritarian
   d. ——hedonist

BOY

1. Birth date: ————————————
2. I.Q. (K.A.): ————————(if more than one, record)
3. School promotion: ——no information
   ——normal   ——retarded once   ——retarded more than once

4. Birth conditions: ——no information
   a. ——normal   d. ——premature
   b. ——instrument; no record of injury   e. ——Caesarean
   c. ——instrument; record of injury

5. Neurological difficulties
   ——yes   ——some indication   ——none recorded

6. Enuresis: ——insufficient record of childhood
   ——none noted   ——some   ——abnormal

7. Health (check all that are applicable):
   a. ——very bad tonsils   e. ——overweight
   b. ——glandular disorder   f. ——undernourished
   c. ——severe acne   g. ——stomach (digestive) trouble
   d. ——body deformity

8. Oral tendencies (check all that are applicable):
   a. ——prolonged thumb sucking   c. ——excessive smoking
   b. ——playing with mouth   d. ——eating orgies

9. Body care: ——no indication
   ——excessive   ——normal   ——inadequate (e.g., very sloppy)

10. Energy level (childhood):   ——no indication
   ——hyperactive   ——normal   ——passive

11. Church attendance: ——no mention
   ——regular   ——irregular   ——no church attendance

12. Primary reference group: ——no indication
   a. ——home   d. ——alternating: delinquent,
   b. ——nondelinquent peers   nondelinquent
   c. ——delinquent peer group

13. Attitude toward mother: ——no indication
   a. ——idealized   c. ——disapproving or disdainful
   b. ——favorable   d. ——fearful

(boy)

14. Attitude toward father:　——no indication
   a. ——idealized　　　c. ——disapproving or disdainful
   b. ——favorable　　　d. ——fearful

15. Reaction to problems:　——no information
   ——accepts and attempts to solve　　——escapes

16. Attitude:　——no indication
   a. ——very self-confident
   b. ——moderately self-confident
   c. ——strong inferiority complex

17. Personality:　——no indication
   ——extrovert　　——introvert　　——neither

18. Desire for adult approval:　——no indication
   ——strong　　——moderate　　——weak

19. Anxiety about sex:　——no indication
   ——apparently none　　——some　　——strong

20. Pattern of sexual experience:　——no information
   a. ——premature (heterosexual)　c. ——excessive masturbation
   b. ——abnormal　　　d. ——apparently normal

21. Femininity:　——no indication
   a. ——evidence of abnormal homosexual activities
   b. ——marked feminine tendencies
   c. ——normally masculine or slight feminine tendencies

22. Suicidal tendencies:　——no information
   a. ——actual suicidal attempts　c. ——suggestion of suicidal
   b. ——frequent suicidal threats　　　tendencies
   d. ——apparently none

23. Aggressiveness:　——no indication
   ——unrestrained　　——moderate　　——greatly inhibited

24. Destructive tendencies:　——no indication
   ——strong sadism　　——strong masochism　　——neither

25. Feelings of grandiosity:　——no indication
   ——none　　——some　　——psychotic

26. Fantasies:　——no information
   a. ——dependency　　　c. ——popularity or success
   b. ——aggression or power　d. ——suicidal

27. Perceived problems within home:　————————————

28. Abnormal fears:　——no information
   ——yes　　——apparently none

29. Group behavior:　——no information
   a. ——a leader
   b. ——seldom a leader; participates in group activities
   c. ——does not participate in group activities

30. Relations with peers: ——no indication
        ——very aggressive   ——cooperative   ——very withdrawn

| Counselor | Dates | Intensity* | | Relation† | | Focus‡ |
		boy	family	boy	family	
_____	_____	__	__	__	__	__
_____	_____	__	__	__	__	__
_____	_____	__	__	__	__	__
_____	_____	__	__	__	__	__

* A: every other week (6 mo. minimum)   ‡ 1: academic
   B: once a month (1 year minimum)   2: medical
   C: less often   3: group participation
† D: close   4: personal problems
   E: friendly   5: family counselor
   F: distant

APPENDIX II

RELIABILITY OF THE CATEGORIZATIONS

A check on inter-rater agreement was conducted on thirty cases randomly selected from the 255 boys who formed the original "treatment" group of the Cambridge-Somerville Youth Study and whose records were used for this analysis of alcoholism. For the reliability check, a second reader read and rated each of the thirty cases. Then the two ratings were compared and the per cent of agreement in categorizing each variable for the thirty cases was computed. For instances in which there was disagreement in categorization, the two raters discussed the case and came to agreement. "Per cent of agreement" reflects, of course, the original ratings.

The per cents of agreement for the various categories ranged from a low of 60 per cent to a high of 100 per cent. Naturally, there is a greater probability of achieving high inter-rater agreement as the number of possible choices decreases. Thus, we were faced with the problem of assessing the per cents of agreement in terms of their likelihood of occurring by chance.

Two formulas were suggested to us: one based upon the number of classifications available for each rating, and one based upon the final distribution of the population among the classifications. Briefly, the arguments for each are presented below.

On the one hand, one can argue that "chance" should be based solely upon the number of categories available—for if each rater were to check blindly or mechanically, he would be as likely to select one as another (regardless of their applicability).

Edward Martin Bennett et al. have presented a formula* based upon this argument to check the probability that observed agreement was in excess of chance agreement: $S = [K/(K-1)](Po - 1/K)$. In this formula, Po represents the per cent agreement between the raters and K represents the number of available categories. (Thus, $1/K$ is "chance" agreement.)

On the other hand, William A. Scott† has argued that there might

---

*Edward Martin Bennett et al., "Communications Through Limited-Response Questioning," *Public Opinion Quarterly,* Vol. 18, Fall, 1954.

† William A. Scott, "Reliability of Content Analysis: The Case of Nominal Scale Coding," *ibid.,* Vol. 19, Fall, 1955.

not be equal probability for the selection of any one of the available categories. He suggests that a researcher need only add meaningless or irrelevant categories to his ratings in order to increase the apparent reliability of inter-rater agreement. Agreement between two raters would be more easily obtained for ratings of a skewed population (e.g., our rating of homosexuality).

Scott's formula incorporates the final distribution of ratings in its estimate of chance agreement: $\pi = (Po - Pe)/(1 - Pe)$. In this formula, Po represents the per cent agreement between raters and Pe is computed by summing the squares of the proportion of the 255 cases as they were distributed in the final ratings for each variable.

We have left to the reader the choice between these arguments. In the following pages, we present both S (in which equal probability among available categories is assumed) and π (in which "chance" is assumed to vary according to final distribution of the ratings).

We have included all variables mentioned in the text and some additional measures, none of which was significantly related to alcoholism, which might be of interest to the reader. The variables have been somewhat arbitrarily grouped under headings which, we hope, will facilitate reference. Both π and S may be interpreted as the extent to which the coding reliability exceeds chance.

	Per Cent Agreement (N: 30)	S	π
The family			
Neighborhood	96.7	.950	.930
Cultural background	100.0	1.000	1.000
Number of children	93.3	.927	.924
Sex deviance	90.0	.875	.479
Parental dominance	83.3	.791	.762
Parental affection	70.0	.625	.617
Parental conflict	75.3	.644	.647
Conflict about alcohol	83.3	.777	.755
The mother			
Age at birth of boy	100.0	1.000	1.000
Number of husbands	93.3	.911	.676
Education	90.0	.851	.833
Ethnic maladjustment	86.7	.801	.832
Religion	76.7	.709	.678
Employment outside home	90.0	.867	.808
Social involvement	80.0	.733	.664
Stomach trouble	96.7	.951	.905
Absence from home	100.0	1.000	1.000
Deviance	86.7	.852	.691
Sex anxiety	80.0	.733	.664
Reaction to crises	66.7	.630	.584
Amount of drinking	83.3	.777	.665
Attitude toward drinking	83.3	.777	.656
Aggressiveness	90.0	.867	.784

	Per Cent Agreement (N: 30)	S	π
Esteem for husband	90.0	.851	.833
Role in family	73.3	.679	.532
Attitude toward son	83.3	.799	.757
Control of son	80.0	.733	.709
Encouragement of dependency	80.0	.701	.633
Encouragement of masculine behavior	86.7	.823	.759
Technique of discipline	83.3	.799	.772

The father

Birthplace	100.0	1.000	1.000
Occupation	93.3	.911	.872
Regularity of employment	93.3	.911	.890
Age at birth of boy	96.7	.962	.961
Education	86.7	.851	.837
Ethnic maladjustment	90.0	.851	.825
Religion	90.0	.886	.856
Social involvement	80.0	.733	.725
Stomach trouble	93.3	.900	.860
Absence from home	96.7	.934	.903
Deviance	86.7	.852	.827
Reaction to crises	73.3	.703	.678
Amount of drinking	80.0	.733	.735
Attitude toward drinking	73.3	.644	.478
Aggressiveness	76.7	.689	.619
Esteem for wife	80.0	.701	.597
Role in family	73.3	.666	.632
Grandiosity	73.3	.644	.567
Self-confidence	80.0	.733	.729
Masculinity	70.0	.625	.514
Value emphasis	60.0	.520	.424
Attitude toward son	76.7	.720	.710
Technique of discipline	66.7	.600	.581

The boy

Relative position in family	100.0	1.000	1.000
Sex of siblings	100.0	1.000	1.000
Relation to siblings	76.7	.720	.693
Nature of birth	96.7	.960	.881
I.Q.	97.7	.964	.972
Neurological difficulties	93.3	.900	.846
Glandular disorder	93.3	.866	.687
Nutritional deficiency	100.0	1.000	1.000
School promotion	96.7	.956	.945
Enuresis	90.0	.867	.803
Energy level	76.7	.689	.598
Oral tendencies	93.3	.923	.852
Femininity	80.0	.733	.333
Extroversion	86.7	.823	.798

Self-confidence	80.0	.733	.623
Psychosomatic symptoms	93.3	.433	.721
Suicidal tendencies	80.0	.750	.265
Abnormal fears	93.3	.900	.880
Desire for adult approval	70.0	.600	.525
Aggressiveness	86.7	.823	.776
Destructiveness	93.3	.911	.828
Group participation	76.7	.689	.588
Relations with peers	86.7	.823	.650
Attitude toward mother	86.7	.834	.741
Attitude toward father	73.3	.666	.630
Significant outsider	86.7	.823	.714
How compared to others	63.3	.541	.525
Expectations or demands	70.0	.600	.535
Amount of supervision	83.3	.777	.710
Use of threats	83.3	.750	.734
Primary disciplinarian (in childhood)	80.0	.767	.627

APPENDIX III

ALCOHOLISM IN THE CONTROL GROUP

Our analyses were based on the 255 boys who were members of the "treatment" group of the Cambridge-Somerville Youth Study. These boys and their families had been observed, on the average, for more than five years in their daily activities. A second set of 255 boys, originally matched to the treatment cases, comprised the "control group" of the experiment. Records about these boys were limited to a physical and psychological examination at the beginning of the project, interviews with the boys' mothers, teachers' reports, and a follow-up interview with each boy in 1948. Thus, the information on this group was comparatively meager and less detailed, and it had been gathered through formal interviews.

For the group whose records were based on observations, we were able to make some rather fine distinctions (e.g., those between ambivalence and rejection). Many of these distinctions were fruitful in analyzing the causes of alcoholism. Such distinctions, the authors believe, could not be made with adequate validity on the basis of intermittent interviews. Furthermore, there are strong indications that "interview biases" mar the validity of data obtained in the control group interviews.*

Nevertheless, the control group does provide a sample of prealcoholics quite comparable in social class, ethnic background, and rates of deviance in adulthood to the treatment group. Therefore, despite the important defects in their records, we computed alcoholism rates among the control boys for variables that were significantly related to alcoholism among the treatment group. We present these figures in the following pages.†

A. *Predisposing Factors:* The three predisposing factors measured by observations were related as expected when the ratings were based on

---

* Joan McCord and William McCord, "Cultural Stereotypes and the Validity of Interviews for Research in Child Development," *Child Development* (in press).

† Criminals and subjects arrested only once for drunkenness were omitted from all analyses. The remaining sample numbered 189. The tables omit subjects about whom no rating could be made.

interviews; none of the differences, however, were significant with a confidence level of $P < .05$.

	Per Cent Who Became Alcoholics
Sexual deviance in family	
Incest or illegitimacy known to have occurred (N: 15)	27
Neither known to have occurred (N: 174)	10
Parental conflict	
Little (N: 59)	8
Some (N: 57)	9
Intense (N: 39)	15
Mother's religion	
Strong Catholic (N: 67)	10
Weak Catholic (N: 44)	14
Strong Protestant (N: 28)	0
Weak Protestant (N: 39)	15

B. Dependency Conflict: Each of the variables shows a trend in the same direction as the ratings based on interviews; only the mother's role in the family is significant at the .05 level of confidence.

	Per Cent Who Became Alcoholics
Mother's attitude toward son	
Warm (N: 88)	8
Passive (N: 91)	11
Rejecting (N: 12)	25
Mother's reaction to crises	
Unrealistic (N: 38)	11
Realistic (N: 44)	7
Mother's deviance	
Deviant (N: 14)	21
Nondeviant (N: 161)	11
Father's esteem for wife	
Low (N: 26)	15
Moderate or high (N: 104)	12
Parental affection	
Affectionate (N: 84)	10
Indifferent (N: 11)	9
Antagonistic (N: 32)	19
Mother's role in family ($P < .05$)	
Leader (N: 116)	11
Passive (N: 26)	4
Ambiguous (N: 29)	21

C. Role Confusion: The interviews gave no indication of parental demands or of the presence of an outsider whose influence was contrary to that of the parents. We therefore had no ratings of those factors. Among the remaining variables in the ratings linked with role confusion, the trends were in the expected direction. Only one, however, was significant beyond the .05 level of confidence: A significantly higher proportion of the men whose fathers had been deviants became alcoholics.

	Per Cent Who Became Alcoholics
Father's birthplace	
Immigrant (N: 95)	8
Native-born (N: 88)	15
Father's reaction to crises	
Unrealistic (N: 51)	14
Realistic (N: 24)	8
Paternal deviance (P < .02)	
Alcoholic (N: 40)	18
Nonalcoholic, deviant (N: 16)	31
Nondeviant (N: 112)	8
Mother's restrictiveness	
Overly restrictive (N: 36)	5
Normally restrictive (N: 104)	12
Subnormally restrictive (N: 42)	14
Supervision of boy	
Present (N: 111)	8
Sporadic or absent (N: 75)	16

D. The Prealcoholic: Unfortunately, there were no measures for the control group on the prealcoholic's relations to his siblings, his abnormal fears, or his sadism. Among the measures of the prealcoholics that were obtainable from the interviews and teachers' reports, we found some significant relationships that did not appear among the observed group. The general picture of the prealcoholic in the control group is, however, essentially similar to the one we obtained of the treatment group: The pre-alcoholics were apparently independent, aggressive, and anxious.

a) The prealcoholic's attitude toward his mother tended to be disapproving. For the treatment group, this difference was significant; there was a nonsignificant trend in the same direction among the control boys:

	Per Cent Who Became Alcoholics
Boy's attitude toward mother	
Favorable (N: 146)	11
Unfavorable (N: 11)	18

b) The prealcoholics were apparently self-confident; they were less likely to display strong feelings of inferiority. This difference was significant for the boys both in the treatment and in the control groups.

	Per Cent Who Became Alcoholics
Boy's self-confidence (P < .05)	
Very self-confident (N: 22)	18
Moderately self-confident (N: 112)	11
Strong feelings of inferiority (N: 67)	3

c) The prealcoholics tended to be extroverts in childhood. This difference was significant for the control boys, though not for the treatment boys.

Per Cent Who Be-
came Alcoholics

Boy's extroversion (P < .05)
Extrovert (N: 79) 19
Introvert (N: 53) 6

d) The prealcoholics tended to participate in group activities during childhood. This difference was significant for the control boys, though not for the treatment boys.

Per Cent Who Be-
came Alcoholics

Group participation (P < .005)
Generally participates (N: 141) 13
Rarely participates (N: 41) 2

e) The prealcoholics tended not to show a strong desire for adult approval. This difference was significant for the control boys, though not for the treatment boys.

Per Cent Who Be-
came Alcoholics

Boy's desire for adult approval (P < .02)
Strong (N: 65) 3
Moderate (N: 74) 12
Weak (N: 16) 31

f) The prealcoholics tended to be highly aggressive. This finding was significant for both the treatment and the control boys.

Per Cent Who Be-
came Alcoholics

Boy's aggressiveness (P < .005)
Unrestrained (N: 32) 28
Moderate (N: 95) 12
Inhibited (N: 42) 2

g) The prealcoholics tended to be hyperactive. This finding was significant for both the treatment and the control boys.

Per Cent Who Be-
came Alcoholics

Boy's energy level (P < .05)
Hyperactive (N: 46) 20
Normal or passive (N: 139) 9

The reliability of ratings for the interviews was based on a random sample of twenty-five cases. See Appendix II for a description of Bennett's S formula and Scott's π formula. Both π and S may be interpreted as the extent to which the coding reliability exceeds chance.

RELIABILITY OF RATINGS FOR THE CONTROL GROUP

	Per Cent Agreement (N: 25)	S	π
Sexual deviance in family	100.0	1.000	1.000
Parental conflict	68.0	.573	.578
Mother's religion	100.0	1.000	1.000
Mother's attitude toward son	96.0	.947	.940
Mother's reaction to crises	80.0	.754	.699
Mother's deviant behavior	100.0	1.000	1.000
Father's esteem for wife	96.0	.947	.699
Parental affection	80.0	.750	.735
Mother's role in family	76.0	.713	.622
Father's birthplace	100.0	1.000	1.000
Father's reaction to crises	72.0	.689	.557
Father's deviant behavior	84.0	.822	.758
Mother's restrictiveness	96.0	.947	.913
Supervision of boy	92.0	.893	.870
Boy's attitude toward mother	72.0	.650	.433
Boy's self-confidence	76.0	.680	.603
Boy's extroversion	76.0	.680	.656
Boy's group participation	84.0	.787	.695
Boy's desire for adult approval	68.0	.573	.544
Boy's aggressiveness	76.0	.680	.597
Boy's energy level	88.0	.840	.820

NOTES TO CHAPTERS

NOTES TO CHAPTER 1

1. Edwin Powers and Helen Witmer, *An Experiment in the Prevention of Delinquency* (New York, Columbia University Press, 1950).

2. William McCord and Joan McCord (in collaboration with Irving Kenneth Zola), *Origins of Crime* (New York, Columbia University Press, 1959).

3. More comprehensive descriptions of the early history of the Cambridge-Somerville project can be found in the works cited in notes 1 and 2.

4. Expert Committee on Mental Health (Alcoholism), "Report on the Second Session, October 15–20, 1951" (Mimeographed, Geneva, World Health Organization, November 1951).

5. M. Keller and V. Efron, "Alcoholism," *Encyclopedia Americana*, I, 348.

6. A check in 1948 indicated that 92 per cent of the sample were still living in the Boston area.

7. The probable biases affecting information in the control group are discussed in Joan McCord and William McCord, "Cultural Stereotypes and the Use of Interviews in Research on Child Development," *Child Development* (in press).

8. Alcoholic, noncriminal; alcoholic, criminal; explosive drinker, noncriminal; explosive drinker, criminal; criminal, nonalcoholic; none of these.

9. There is, of course, an extensive debate going on among statistical experts concerning the usefulness of the Chi-square test and other measures of significance. For the reader who puts faith in tests of significance, we have presented their results; other readers can dismiss them and concentrate on the raw figures converted to per cents.

10. John D. Armstrong, "The Search for the Alcoholic Personality," *The Annals of the American Academy of Political and Social Science: Understanding Alcoholism*, Vol. 315 (January 1958), edited by Seldon D. Bacon.

11. Another longitudinal study of alcoholism has been initiated. The first results will be reported in Patricia O'Neal and Lee N. Robins, "Adult Drinking Behavior of Problem Children," a chapter in the forthcoming anthology, *Society, Culture, and Drinking Patterns* (edited by David J. Pittman and Charles Snyder). Although the research concentrates on a different type of sample (children who were voluntary patients at a St. Louis mental health clinic), it is encouraging to note that its basic findings—although not the interpretation—resemble ours.

NOTES TO CHAPTER 2

1. Benjamin Rush, "An Inquiry into the Effects of Ardent Spirits Upon the Human Body and Mind," *Quarterly Journal of Studies on Alcohol*, Vol. 4, Sept. 1943, p. 327.

2. Roger J. Williams, "The Genetotrophic Concept—Nutritional Deficiencies and Alcoholism," *Annals of the New York Academy of Science*, Vol. 57, 1954, pp. 794–811.

3. Roger J. Williams, "The Etiology of Alcoholism: A Working Hypothesis Involving the Interplay of Hereditary and Environmental Factors," *Quarterly Journal of Alcoholism*, Vol. 7, March 1947, pp. 567–87.

4. Jorge Madrones, Natividad Segorua, Arturo Hederra, "Heredity of Experimental Alcohol Preference in Rats," *Quarterly Journal*, Vol. 14, No. 1, March 1953.

5. Cited in Carney Landis, "Theories of the Alcoholic Personality," *Alcohol, Science and Society, Quarterly Journal*, New Haven, 1945.

6. M. Freile Fleetwood, in Oskar Diethelm, *The Etiology of Chronic Alcoholism*, Springfield, Ill., Charles C Thomas, 1955.

7. J. W. Tintera and H. W. Lovell, "Endocrine Treatment of Alcoholism," *Geriatrics*, Vol. 4, 1949, pp. 274–80.

8. James J. Smith, "The Endocrine Basis and Hormonal Therapy of Alcoholism," *New York State Journal of Medicine*, Vol. 50, 1950, pp. 1704–6, 1711–15.

9. Manfred Bleuler, "Familial and Personal Background of Chronic Alcoholics," in Oskar Diethelm, *The Etiology of Chronic Alcoholism*.

10. X^2 3.69; d.f. 1 (corrected for small N).

11. E. M. Jellinek, "Heredity of the Alcoholic," in *Alcohol*, note 5.

12. Manfred Bleuler, note 9.

13. Ann Roe, "Children of Alcoholic Parents Raised in Foster Homes," *Alcohol*, note 5.

14. Karl Menninger, *Man Against Himself*, New York, Harcourt, Brace, and Co., 1938, p. 149.

15. Otto Fenichel, *The Psychoanalytic Theory of Neurosis*, New York, W. W. Norton Co., 1945.

16. Giorgio Lolli, "Alcoholism as a Disorder of the Love Disposition," *Quarterly Journal*, Vol. 17, No. 1, March 1956, pp. 96–107.

17. Alan D. Button, "The Genesis and Development of Alcoholism: An Empirically Based Schema," *Quarterly Journal*, Vol. 1, No. 4, Dec. 1956, pp. 671–75.

18. Sandor Ferenczi, "Alkohol und Neurosis," *Jahrbuch für psychoanalytische Forschungen*, 1911.

19. Cited in Otto Fenichel, *The Psychoanalytical Theory of Neurosis*, pp. 366–86.

20. J. V. Quaranta, "Alcoholism: A Study of Emotional Maturity and Homosexuality as Related Factors in Compulsive Drinking," Fordham University thesis, 1947.

21. Carney Landis, *Alcohol, Science and Society*.

22. Heinz and Rowena Ansbacher, *The Individual Psychology of Alfred Adler*, New York, Basic Books, 1956, p. 423.

23. X^2 4.78; d.f. 1 (comparison of marked inferiority feelings to moderate inferiority feelings and superiority feelings).

24. Ansbacher, *The Individual Psychology of Alfred Adler*, p. 423.

25. Robert White, *The Abnormal Personality*, New York, Ronald Press, 1948, p. 417.

26. Albert D. Ullman, "Sociocultural Backgrounds of Alcoholism," *The Annals of the American Academy of Political and Social Science: Understanding Alcoholism*, Vol. 315 (January 1958), p. 50.

27. R. F. Bales, "Cultural Differences in Rates of Alcoholism," *Quarterly Journal*, Vol. 6, March 1946, p. 482.

28. *Ibid.*, p. 493.

29. Charles Snyder, *Alcohol and the Jews*, Yale Center of Alcohol Studies, 1958.

30. Charles R. Snyder and Ruth H. Landman, "Studies of Drinking in Jewish Culture," *Quarterly Journal*, Vol. 12, pp. 451–75; Vol. 13, pp. 87–95; Vol. 16, pp. 101–78, 263–90, 504–33, 700–742; and Vol. 17, pp. 124–43.

31. Giorgio Lolli, "The Use of Wine and Other Alcoholic Beverages by a Group of Italians and Americans of Italian Extraction," *Quarterly Journal*, Vol. 13, March 1952, pp. 27–49.

32. Phyllis H. Williams and Robert Straus, "Drinking Patterns of Italians in New Haven: Utilization of the Personal Diary as a Research Technique," *Quarterly Journal*, March and Sept., 1952, and Sept. 1953.

33. Milton L. Barnett, "Alcoholism in the Cantonese of New York City: An Anthropological Study," in Diethelm, *The Etiology of Chronic Alcoholism*.

34. Jerome H. Skolnick, "A Study of the Relation of Ethnic Background to Arrests for Inebriety," *Quarterly Journal*, No. 4, Dec. 1954, pp. 622–30.

35. David Horton, "The Functions of Alcohol in Primitive Societies: A Cross-Cultural Study," *Quarterly Journal of Studies on Alcohol*, Vol. 4, 1943, pp. 199–320.

36. X^2 6.63; d.f. 1.

37. Seldon Bacon, "Social Settings Conducive to Alcoholism: A Sociological Approach to a Medical Problem," *Journal of the American Medical Association*, Vol. 164, Bay 11, 1957, pp. 179 ff.

38. The number of cases in this chart is smaller than in the previous one, for it was not always possible to establish the birthplace of the fathers.

39. X^2 4.9; d.f. 1.

40. John Dollard, "Drinking Mores of the Social Classes," pp. 95–104 in *Alcohol*, note 5.

41. X^2 4.95.

42. John W. Riley and Charles F. Marden, "The Social Pattern of Alcoholic Drinking," *Quarterly Journal*, Vol. 8, pp. 265–73.

43. Joan K. Jackson and Ralph Conner, "Attitudes of the Parents of Alcoholics, Moderate Drinkers and Non-drinkers Toward Drinking," *Quarterly Journal*, Vol. 14, pp. 590–613.

44. Albert D. Ullman, "The First Drinking Experience of Addictive and of Normal Drinkers," *Quarterly Journal*, 1953, Vol. 14, pp. 181–91.

NOTES TO CHAPTER 3

1. X^2 5.9; d.f. 1.   2. X^2 3.01; d.f. 1, corrected for small N.

3. X^2 8.20; d.f. 1, corrected for small N (an equally high rate of alcoholism was found in families characterized by incest as in those characterized by illegitimacy).

4. X^2 6.1; d.f. 1.
5. X^2 6.9; d.f. 1 (none or some).
6. X^2 9.8; d.f. 1, corrected for small N.

NOTES TO CHAPTER 4

1. X^2 11.7; d.f. 2. Comparing alternating mothers to affectionate and rejecting mothers: X^2 6.1, corrected for small N.
2. X^2 14.2; d.f. 2.   3. X^2 5.7; d.f. 1, corrected for small N.
4. X^2 5.9; d.f. 1, corrected for small N.
5. X^2 5.6; d.f. 1.   6. X^2 17.9; d.f. 2.
7. X^2 12.5; d.f. 1, corrected for small N.
8. X^2 3.9; d.f. 1, corrected for small N.
9. X^2 8.5; d.f. 1.   10. X^2 9.3; d.f. 1, corrected for small N.
11. X^2 4.1; d.f. 1.   12. X^2 7.4; d.f. 1.
13. X^2 6.0; d.f. 1.   14. X^2 9.8; d.f. 1, corrected for small N.

NOTES TO CHAPTER 5

1. X^2 6.1; d.f. 1.   2. X^2 5.2; d.f. 1.   3. X^2 10.9; d.f. 2.
4. X^2 7.8; d.f. 1.   5. X^2 10.3; d.f. 1, corrected for small N.
6. X^2 4.4; d.f. 1.   7. X^2 7.4; d.f. 1, corrected for small N.
8. X^2 4.4; d.f. 1.   9. X^2 10.5; d.f. 1, corrected for small N.
10. X^2 11.8 ; d.f. 1.

NOTES TO CHAPTER 6

1. X^0 6.8; d.f. 1.   2. X^2 5.0; d.f. 1. Fathers who deserted the home were included as escapist.   3. X^2 7.0; d.f. 2.
4. X^2 10.3; d.f. 2.   5. X^2 7.1; d.f. 1.   6. X^2 14.3; d.f. 2.
7. X^2 15.3; d.f. 2. Comparison of moderate or high to low among not actively affectionate mothers, X^2 4.4; d.f. 1.
8. X^2 47.3; d.f. 2.   9. X^2 58.0; d.f. 2.
10. Since only 15.5 per cent of the sample were alcoholics, a prediction that none would become alcoholic would have been 84.5 per cent correct. 93 per cent accuracy is, however, significantly better than this estimate of chance. (X^2 5.8; d.f. 1).

NOTES TO CHAPTER 7

1. Perhaps it should be noted that a relatively small proportion of the alcoholic criminals could be classified as sex criminals.
2. William McCord and Joan McCord (with Irving Kenneth Zola), *Origins of Crime.* New York, Columbia University Press, 1959. Criminality was more broadly defined in that work and many of the alcoholics in the present study were classified as criminal in the former.
3. X^2 8.9; d.f. 1. Criminals compared to nondeviants.
4. X^2 4.8; d.f. 1, corrected for small N. Criminals compared to nondeviants.

5. X^2 10.6. Criminals compared to nondeviants.
6. X^2 8.7; d.f. 1, corrected for small N. Criminals compared to nondeviants.
7. X^2 11.6; d.f. 1. Criminals compared to nondeviants.
8. X^2 8.5; d.f. 1. Alcoholics compared to nondeviants.
9. X^2 12.9; d.f. 1. Criminals compared to nondeviants.
10. X^2 7.1; d.f. 1, corrected for small N. Deviants compared to nondeviants.
11. X^2 14.9; d.f. 1. Deviants compared to nondeviants.
12. X^2 6.7; d.f. 1. Deviants compared to nondeviants.
13. X^2 6.2; d.f. 1. Criminals compared to nondeviants.
14. X^2 5.5; d.f. 1, corrected for small N. Alcoholics compared to nondeviants.
15. X^2 7.8; d.f. 1. Criminals compared to nondeviants.
16. X^2 11.4; d.f. 2. Criminals compared to nondeviants.
17. X^2 4.4; d.f. 1. Alcoholics compared to criminals.
18. X^2 9.5; d.f. 1. Criminals compared to nondeviants.
19. X^2 4.2; d.f. 1. Criminals compared to nondeviants.
20. X^2 5.2; d.f. 1. Alcoholics compared to criminals.
21. X^2 3.8; d.f. 1. Criminals compared to nondeviants.
22. X^2 6.1; d.f. 1. Criminals compared to nondeviants.
23. X^2 4.8; d.f. 1. Alcoholics compared to criminals.
24. X^2 15.2; d.f. 2. Criminals compared to nondeviants.
25. X^2 7.5; d.f. 1. Criminals compared to nondeviants.
26. X^2 14.0; d.f. 1. Criminals compared to nondeviants.
27. X^2 5.3; d.f. 1. Alcoholics compared to nondeviants.
28. X^2 8.0; d.f. 1. Criminals compared to nondeviants.
29. X^2 9.69; d.f. 1, corrected for small N. Criminals compared to nondeviants.
30. X^2 9.8; d.f. 1. Criminals compared to nondeviants.
31. X^2 8.4; d.f. 1. Criminals compared to nondeviants.
32. Fisher test, one-tailed.
33. X^2 17.2; d.f. 1. Criminals compared to nondeviants.
34. Fisher test, one-tailed.
35. X^2 19.4; d.f. 1. Criminals compared to nondeviants.
36. X^2 4.2; d.f. 1. Criminals compared to nondeviants.
37. Fisher test, one-tailed.
38. X^2 4.52; d.f. 1, corrected for small N. Alcoholics compared to criminals.
39. Fisher test, one-tailed.
40. X^2 4.5; d.f. 1. Criminals compared to nondeviants. Among boys reared in transitional neighborhoods, however, criminality was significantly less likely to occur if the mother was affectionate: X^2 4.30; d.f. 1 (criminals compared to nondeviants).
41. X^2 5.9; d.f. 1. The difference between criminal and noncriminal alcoholics is nonsignificant, but suggestive.
42. See Joan McCord and William McCord, "The Effects of Paternal Role Model on Criminality," *Journal of Social Issues*, Vol. XIV, No. 3, 1958.
43. Recently, we have analyzed the background of functional psychotics within the Cambridge-Somerville sample. It should be noted, in passing, that

the psychotics differed from both the alcoholics *and* the criminals. The psychotics had typically been raised in an environment characterized by a dominant, overprotective, and affectionate mother and by a passive, emotionally distant father. This research is reported in "The Familial Origins of Psychoses," by William McCord, Judith Porta, and Joan McCord, in preparation.

NOTES TO CHAPTER 8

1. Carney Landis, "Theories of the Alcoholic Personality," *Alcohol, Science, and Society, Quarterly Journal of Studies on Alcohol,* New Haven, 1945.

2. Leonard Syme, "Personality Characteristics of the Alcoholic," *Quarterly Journal of Studies on Alcohol,* Vol. 18, 1957.

3. John D. Armstrong, "The Search for the Alcoholic Personality," *The Annals of the American Academy of Political and Social Science,* January 1958.

4. Armstrong, *ibid.,* p. 45.   5. X^2 24.05; d.f. 2.   6. X^2 9.19; d.f. 2.

7. X^2 19.54; d.f. 4. Comparing only affectionate fathers we found that alcoholics were significantly more likely to be passive in expressing their affection: X^2 4.4.   8. X^2 24.3; d.f. 2.   9. X^2 11.3; d.f. 1.

10. X^2 66.61; d.f. 2.   11. X^2 15.06; d.f. 4.

12. William McCord and Joan McCord (with Irving Kenneth Zola), *Origins of Crime.* New York, Columbia University Press, 1959.

13. X^2 26.10; d.f. 2.   14. X^2 8.30; d.f. 1.

15. X^2 46.2; d.f. 2: "popularity" and "achievement" omitted because of small number of cases.   16. X^2 29.92; d.f. 2.

17. X^2 7.97; d.f. 1 ("Dependent" *versus* others). X^2 6.8; d.f. 2.

18. X^2 5.22; d.f. 1, corrected for small N.

19. X^2 5.4; d.f. 1 ("Indifferent" *versus* all others).

20. X^2 4.8; d.f. 1.   21. X^2 4.15; d.f. 1.   22. X^2 8.52; d.f. 2.

23. X^2 4.77; d.f. 1, corrected for small N.   24. X^2 3.2; d.f. 1.

25. X^2 4.0; d.f. 1.

26. Several other measures indicated the pre-alcoholics' tendency to appear "manly" and independent; they were, for example, more likely to reject their home as a primary reference group and they more often *avoided* behavior oriented to gaining direct approval from adults. These other differences were not, however, statistically significant.

NOTES TO CHAPTER 9

1. Ruth Fox and Peter Lyon, *Alcoholism,* New York, Random House, 1955.

2. *Ibid.,* pp. 108–9.

3. Harold Maine, *If a Man Be Mad,* London, Victor Gollancz, 1952, p. 94.

4. *Ibid.,* p. 18.   5. *Ibid.,* p. 132.   6. *Ibid.,* p. 133.

INDEX

Abraham, Karl, 31
Adler, Alfred, 32–34 *passim*
Armstrong, John D., 124–25
Aggression: in family background, 115–18; of adult alcoholics, 132; of pre-alcoholics, 137
Aggression in child's environment and type of deviance, 115–18
Alcohol: functions of, 54, 56, 70, 155; American attitude toward, 156–57
Alcoholism: definition, 9–12; operational definition, 10–11; rates in treatment and control groups, 13; physiological theories of, 22–28; hereditary theories of, 26; psychological theories of, 28; sociological theories of, 35–43; prediction, 94–95. *See also* rates, parental deviance
Alcoholics Anonymous, x, 10, 156
Allport, Gordon, ix
Anxiety, 136, 138; sexual, 138
Armstrong, John D., 19, 124
Attitude toward parents of alcoholics, 135

Bacon, Seldon, 39
Bales, Robert F., 36
Barnett, Milton, 37
Bennett, Edward, 176
Bleuler, Manfred, 24, 26
Boston Committee on Alcoholism, x, 10
Button, Alan, 30

Cabot, P. Sidney de Q., 7
Cabot, Richard, x, 6
Cambridge-Somerville Youth Study, history, x, 6–8

Case records, 13–18, 165–74
Catholicism, 51–53, 93; and crime, 112
Causation: of alcoholism, compared to crime, 119–23; concepts of, 145–50
Community participation: of adult alcoholics, 126; of pre-alcoholics, 134
Conflict, *see* parental conflict
Conner, Ralph, 41
Conscience of adult alcoholics, 131
Control group: alcoholism in, 181–82; character of, 183
Crime: causal background compared with alcoholism, 96–122; definition of, 97–98; among alcoholics, 98, 115–18

Dependency: maternal encouragement of, 34, 64; conflict in boy, 54–72, 140–41, 152; needs, 54–56, 87–91, 104–6; conflict cumulative factors, 72, 90; conflict and role confusion, 83; conflict, types of, 88–89; conflict and other factors, 92–95; and crime, 103–6; in adult alcoholics, 132; frustration in adulthood, 159; in the control group, 181
Discipline, 75, 79–80; and maternal restrictiveness, 81; and crime, 107–8, 115–18; and demands on child and crime, 111–12; used by adult alcoholics, 129; use of threats and crime, 117
Dollard, John, 39–40

Ella Lyman Cabot Foundation, ix
Employment of adult alcoholics, 126

neural disorder, 50; and mother's attitudes, 58; and maternal deviance, 62; and crime, 100; of adult alcoholics, 128

Parental deviance: and alcoholism, 27, 50–51, 60–63, 64, 78; and crime, 100, 113–14

Parental drinking, 43

Parental emotional relationships, 65; and crime, 108–9

Parental relation to child, 56–57, 69, 74, 77, 88, 90–91; and crime, 102–3, 103–6, 113, 115–18; of adult alcoholics, 127; and child's attitude toward parents, 136

Parental roles in family, 59–60, 63–66; and crime, 100, 113, 116; of adult alcoholics, 128

Parental reactions to crises, 59–60, 76, 106–7, 111

Parental supervision of child, 81–82

Parental use of threats, 117

Parsons, Talcott, 55

Personality of alcoholics, 124–42

Powers, Edwin, ix, 8

Prediction of alcoholism, 94–95

Protestantism, 51, 86–87

Quaranta, J. V., 31

Rates of alcoholism: cultural differences, 35–40; 85–87; social class differences, 39–40, 85–87, 93, 119–20; male-female, 162–64

Reliability of categorization, 15, 176–78, 184

Religion, 51–53; strength of maternal, 52; strength of paternal, 52; and predisposing factors, 52; and ethnic background, 86; and other factors, 86, 93–95; and crime, 112

Riley, John W., 41

Roe, Ann, 27

Role confusion, 73–82, 140, 153; and cumulative influence of stress, 83; and cumulative influence of dependency conflict, 83; and other

factors, 92–95; and crime, 110–15; in the control group, 181–82

Role specification, 79–82, 110–15

Rush, Benjamin, 22–23

Sadism, 137

Sample: selection, 6–8; records on, 12–19

Scott, William, 176–77

Segorua, Natividad, 23

Self-confidence, 136

Self-destruction, 28–30, 136–37

Self-image of alcoholics, 153, 155, 160

Sexual deviance: and alcoholism, 51; and crime, 100

Sexual factors in alcoholism: latent homosexuality, 31–32, 69; sexual deviance in family, 51; maternal sexual anxiety, 67

Sheldon, William, 23

Skolnick, J., 37–38

Smith, James J., 24

Snyder, Charles, 36

Social class, 39–40; and ethnic groups, 85; and other factors, 93; and crime, 119–20

Strauss, Robert, 37

Stress in the family, 72, 83, 92, 99–103, 152

Subjects: see Sample

Suttie, Ian, 55

Syme, Leonard, 124

Theories of alcoholism: physiological, 22–28; psychological, 28–35; sociological, 35–43

Tintera, J. W., 24

Ullman, Albert D., 36, 41

Values of adult alcoholics, 131

White, Robert, 34–35

Williams, Roger, 23, 25

Williams, Phyllis, 37

Witmer, Helen, 8